THE SCHOLAR
THE BUILDERS REJECTED

W. Bro. J.S.M. WARD

THE SCHOLAR
THE BUILDERS REJECTED

Including

THE ENTERED APPRENTICE'S HANDBOOK

THE FELLOWCRAFTS HANDBOOK

THE MASTER MASON'S HANDBOOK

THE HIGHER DEGREES' HANDBOOK

THE MORAL TEACHINGS OF FREEMASONRY

THE ENTERED APPRENTICE'S HANDBOOK

by W.Bro. J.S.M. WARD

INTRODUCTION

By the Hon. Sir John A. Cockburn

W. Bro. Ward is one of the most able and earnest of Masonic students. He brings to bear on the task of research the mind of a scholar, enriched by extensive reading, much travel and a wide experience of men and affairs. In addition to being a well known author of Masonic Works, he was the Founder of the Masonic Study Society, whose first President was the late Sir Richard Vassar Vassar-Smith, 33 degree, and in whose ranks are to be found many eminent Masonic writers.

Brother Ward has by precept and example led others to become eager explorers in the realms of Masonic truth. The present volume is No. I in a series of studies as to the meaning of our Ritual. It deals with the degree of an Entered Apprentice and is calculated to inspire the younger brethren with the resolve not to content themselves with the outward form of our ceremonies, beautiful though it be, but to gain a knowledge of the indwelling soul of Masonry and to comprehend the deep meaning of the ritual with which they are step by step becoming familiar.

Hence they will learn to regard the Craft not only as a world-spread, civilising medium, nor yet only as the most benevolent of all Institutions, but also as a mine of surpassing wealth in which the Wisdom of the Ages has become embedded and preserved. Bro. Ward at the outset disarms anything like hostile criticism by admitting that many brethren may not find themselves in complete accord with all his conclusions. Indeed, it would be surprising if this were the case.

Like Holy Writ, the Ritual is capable of many interpretations. It is a gradual accretion in which succeeding epochs have left their mark. Evolution takes place under the alternation of forces that make for difference and agreement. The process demands a continual adjustment between these apparently contrary, but in reality complementary factors. Each age sets out to balance any deficiency in the preceding period.

When materialism has been pushed to excess, the tendency is rectified by a spiritual revival. On the other hand, an age in which zeal for the gifts of the spirit has caused neglect of temporal welfare is naturally followed by a renaissance of the just claims of the flesh. The subject matter of Masonry is the relationship between Spirit and Matter, between Heaven and Earth, between God and Man, between the Soul and the Body.

Emphasis is everywhere laid on the necessity of their reconciliation. Consequently to attain the juste milieu emphasis has sometimes to be laid on one side and sometimes on the other. For example, the Cross and the Square, which have now such deeply spiritual significance , were originally signs of Earth, and became respectively, the essential symbols of Christianity and Masonry, because it was necessary to proclaim the fact that professions of piety

7

towards God were idle, unless they bore fruit in kindly relationship between man and man.

Bro. Ward regards the J.W. as representing the body, and the S.W. the soul, although the emblems and jewel of the former are celestial and of the latter terrestrial. The fact is that things divine and human are so interwoven in Masonry as to be inseparable. Duty towards God and towards our neighbour are but different aspects of the same truth. For the Fatherhood of God implies the Brotherhood of Man, and, conversely, he who devotes himself to the service of his fellow creatures proves, through his brotherly relationship, his descent from the Father of All.

The issue of Bro. Ward's series of handbooks cannot fail to accomplish its main object, which is to lead not only juniors, but also those well versed in the ritual, to mark, learn and inwardly digest the significance of the ceremonies, which when properly understood, causes our jewels and emblems to glow with an inner light which infinitely enhances their beauty.

The ready reception which Bro. Ward's books have already received at the hands of the Craft, prove that they meet a recognised requirement as expositions of the character of a ritual with whose external features we are familiar, and in which we take our daily delight.

J.A.C.

The Mysteries

In every race and every clime,
Since the earliest days of Time,
Men have taught the Mystic Quest
Shown the Way to Peace and rest.

Bacchus died, and rose again,
On the golden Asian Plain;
Osiris rose from out the grave,
And thereby mankind did save:
Adonis likewise shed his blood
By the yellow Syrian flood,
Zoroaster brought to birth
Mithra from His Cave of Earth.

And to-day in Christian Lands
We with them can join hands.

J.W.

CHAPTER I.

THE OPENING OF THE FIRST DEGREE.

The W.M. calls the brethren together with one knock so as to remind them that the body must be prepared to obey the higher faculties, for if it is not, no spiritual progress is possible. The first question and answer of the J.W. indicate this quite clearly, for the J.W. represents the body and so he satisfies himself that man's body is on guard against outside influences. The S.W., representing the Soul, next proves that all present have made some progress towards the light.

It is only when this has been achieved that any real advancement becomes possible, and only those who have started can help those who still remain in spiritual darkness. The next series of questions indicates that Man has a seven-fold nature. The Ancient Egyptians held this view , and it is endorsed in Masonry by the fact that it takes seven to make a perfect lodge.

There is also, no doubt, an astrological reference to the seven planets and a connection with stellar worship, but as our system is mainly solar, it is almost impossible to give a logical planetary interpretation to the seven who form a lodge, or to the seven officers. In short, the planetary symbolism has become disorganised by the stress laid on the solar aspect of the three principal officers who rule a lodge. Moreover, the predominance of the solar aspect has emphasised the triune nature of man, and symbolises it in these officers.

Thus it will be seen that too much stress must not be laid on the planets, as represented by the seven officers, and a passing reference to the fact that it is still remembered in the number seven is all that can be logically maintained. Similarly there is merely a hint of the seven-fold nature of man. If ours were a stellar system, then clearly the Tyler would represent the body, the divine spark would be represented by the W.M. , the various officers between would symbolise the various sub-divisions of the non-materials parts of man, such as his astral body, his intellectual faculties, and so forth.

Since, however, our system is solar in the main, we should continue to interpret our symbols from that aspect, making but passing reference to stellar influences when they occur. The duties of the Tyler are considered elsewhere, so we will pass to the I.G. Although in some popular workings he and the other two subordinate officers are not allowed to speak for themselves, the Wardens doing this work, in many other rituals they are allowed to answer the W.M. direct.

The I.G. stands for the power which permits the Soul to enter flesh at any given moment. The Soul may desire to become incarnate, but unless its time has come it is turned back at the threshold, and even if it forces itself into birth it is cut short. Entry into life is not an accident, but ordained of God, Who works through His spiritual as well as through His human agents. Those who saw Maeterlinck's play, "The Blue Bird," will remember that the same idea is dealt with in one of the scenes.

Spiritually, the I.G. represents the warning which must be given to those who attempt, without due caution, to probe into the Mysteries of God. They must neither rush forward hastily, nor, having once started, withdraw suddenly; for, if they do, dire evil will befall. This warning all the Mysteries gave, and it is certain that those who dabble in the so-called occult run grave risks unless they use the utmost caution.

Hence it is absolutely essential that the candidate should be properly prepared before he starts on his quest. The J.D. represents the physical means by which the Soul, represented by the S.W., passes on the inspirations received from the Spirit, the W.M., to the material world. In this sense therefore he represents intelligence, and the five senses of man, whereas the S.D. stands for intuition, whereby the Soul obtains its inspiration from the Divine.

In the ancient operative days these officers no doubt had a practical use, the S.D. being the personal messenger of the Master, who took messages to the S.W., not merely when in Lodge, but when he was at a distance, employed on his task, or possibly when he was resting from his labours, In like manner the S.W. 's deacon was sent by him to find the J.W. The J.W. describes his position in L. and indicates quite clearly that he represents the Sun at noon.

From the operative point of view it must be remembered that Noon has always been, and still is, a workingman's dinner hour, hence the special duty of the J.W. ; but in the spiritual sense, since he stands for the body, it is natural that he should have charge over the body's needs. As he also represents the preservative side of God, his interest in the physical well-being of man is appropriate.

With this in mind the F. C. will realise the significance of the P.W., and its connection with C. and W. , which are the emblems of the God of Vegetation in the more primitive rites. When men evolved, and the solar system of religion developed, the God of Vegetation became the Preserver. This characteristic of the J.W. is emphasised by the upright lines of his plumb, which latter reminds us of water which falls from heaven, and of the cast marks of Vishnu in India.

This aspect of the J.W., as representing the Preserver , is carefully maintained throughout the whole of the three degrees and must never be forgotten. In like manner, the fact that he stands for the body is also maintained throughout. Bearing this in mind , we shall perceive the significance of the fact that the Architect of K.S. 's Temple was the J.W. Finally, bread and water represent the bare necessities, without which mortal life cannot be preserved.

Luxuries, which are obtained when we have acquired worldly possessions, i.e., wealth, lead to the death of the soul, and even of the body, unless employed with the greatest caution. Some masons claim that the J.W. originally sat in the North to mark the Sun at noon, meaning to see, or point

12

out, that it had reached the midheavens. Honestly, I can find no real evidence in support of this view, which likewise places the W.M. in the West and the S.W. in the East. It is due, in my opinion, to a complete misunderstanding of the use of the words "to mark."

This phrase implies that the J.W. is placed on a certain spot to mark the position of the Sun at noon, and not that 'he may see it. In a closed-in building, such as a lodge room was, it would be desirable to mark the three positions of the Sun, for the candidate has to pass through each point in turn, and these three officers, who represent the Sun in its three aspects, would naturally sit in the positions in use in a speculative lodge.

Any arguments adduced from the rituals of the modern Operative Lodges are vitiated by two facts-(I) we have no evidence that this peculiarity is really old (it may be due to Stretton's inventive mind) and (2) the Operatives, if old, would be descended from the Guild Masons and not from the Freemasons ; and this might be a peculiarity of theirs, or deliberately adopted so as to differentiate them from the Freemasons.

That the Guild Masons and Freemasons were quite distinct has been proved as far back as 1913, and the fact is gone into in my other book, "Freemasonry and the Ancient Gods." That the Operatives are not descended direct from the Mediaeval Freemasons is shown by the fact that they have entirely different signs from our own. Thus we need not discuss further the question as to whether the J.W. should be in the North or South.

The S.W., as he indicates in his reply to the W.M., represents the Sun in its setting, and so the Destructive Side of the Deity, or Shiva. He also stands for the Soul. Shiva shall close not only our mortal life, but Time itself. But I have dealt with this side of the S.W. very fully elsewhere. It should be noted, however, that the S.W. is associated with level and horizontal lines , and not with perpendiculars, and here again he follows the Hindu system, for Shiva's caste mark is two or more parallel lines.

As the Great Leveller this is most natural, and it reminds us that in the sight of God all souls are equal, even though in mortal life their stations may appear to differ. Shiva is associated with the element of Fire, whereas Vishnu is associated with Water, and as we see that great care has been taken to maintain the connection between the J.W. and Water, so we find that with us the S.W. is similarly associated with Fire, though perhaps less obviously.

Firstly, his level is of a triangular form with the point upward, the world-wide symbol for Fire. Again, the S.W. 's P.W. has hidden within it the same idea. A smith who works in metals can only do so by the help of fire, and in one ritual this fact is stressed. Thus metals come out from the dark earth, and the Sun sinks in the West into darkness and the grave, as does man. But, by means of fire, man obtains wealth from the metals hidden in the earth, and in like manner the Soul of Man rises refined and purified from the grave by means of the divine fire within.

Moreover, one cannot ignore the fact that there is here a hint of the necessity of the purging fire of remorse to cleanse away our sins. The S. W. is the Soul, the link between mortal life and the Divine Spark , but he acts on instructions from the Spirit; in other words, it is only when God decrees our death that the Soul departs from the body. The W.M. represents, as his words indicate, the creative side of God and the Divine Spirit in Man. He sets us to work on earth, but delegates to another the task of calling us back whence we came.

He represents the male aspect of the Deity, as is shown by the tau crosses, called levels, on his apron, and by his use of the gavel, which represents the same emblem. The Tau Cross is, of course, a phallic symbol and stands for the male and creative aspect in Man. As the three principal officers represent the Sun (a masculine planet) in various phases, it is natural that they should all wield the gavel, but the two wardens are less essentially male than the W.M., as is indicated by the fact that they do not have the tau cross or Master's level on their aprons.

The Spirit, being active, is male; whereas both soul and body, being more or less passive, are female. The feminine side of the S.W. or Soul is deliberately emphasised later-in the first degree-by a reference to the Moon, a feminine planet, the emblem of the Soul and of the psychic nature in man. Nor can we ignore the fact that the West is known as the feminine quarter of the heavens, whereas the East is the masculine; it is also worth noticing that Shiva is often depicted with the moon.

Finally, before declaring the L. open, the W.M. offers up a prayer, thereby reminding us that the Divine Spark in Man, or the Spirit, must turn to the Source of All for aid if it would control body and soul. The three knocks, as distinct from the one knock with which the proceedings started, indicate that the members are about to work for the union and advancement of body, soul and spirit, and not for the body only. But the way in which the three knocks are given show that, as yet, there is no unity between the three elements which constitute Man.

CHAPTER II.

THE TYLER

The first thing that greets the eyes of the aspirant to our Order is a man, whom he soon discovers is called the Tyler, standing in front of the door with a d.n. s.d. in his hand. He naturally wants an answer to the question which actually occurs in a certain famous old ritual, "Why does the Tyler wear a s.d.?"-and the answer is, "To guard the brethren and to hele the Word." Let us consider this answer:- "To guard the brethren. "In certain old rituals of the 18th century we are told that Masons' Lodges formerly met in the open-"on the highest hill or lowest valley, where never dog barked nor cock crew."

Brethren will no doubt have read the interesting article in the "Masonic Record" relating to this state of affairs, but I am bound to say that I do not think that the ordinary mediaeval lodge met in such places. The reference to the cock, together with certain details we possess with regard to those lodges which did meet in the open, (they were mostly in Scotland) indicate that they were not ordinary Craft lodges, but much more probably Templar Lodges.

The Templars in the 18th century claimed to be descended from a body which had been suppressed in the years 1307 to 1314-, and actually prescribed. There was every reason therefore why they should meet in out of the way places, but no such reason existed in the case of a lodge of ordinary Freemasons. That such a phrase should have wandered into a craft ritual from Templary is perfectly natural, but it is not safe to argue from this that all Masonic lodges met under the canopy of heaven.

In those early days, many higher degrees were worked in ordinary Craft Lodges, in a way not permitted to-day; and this may easily account for phrases more appropriate to a Templar Preceptory being found in a Craft working. I might add that until the middle of the 19th century Templar meetings were always called "Encampments," indicating that they were camps held in the open fields.

But in mediaeval times we know that the Freemasons had Lodge buildings, and if they went to a new place to build a church or castle , the first thing they did was to erect a temporary Lodge room, which they attended before starting the day's work. Those interested will find abundant details in Fort Newton's interesting little book, "The Builders." There also it is clearly shown that there were two kinds of masons in those days, and the man who conclusively proved this was not a modern Speculative Freemason.

The two groups were the Freemasons and the Guild Masons. The former were lineal descendents of the Comacine Masons-who, incidentally, knew a certain Masonic Sign-and these men were skilled architects, free to go anywhere. They had a monopoly of ecclesiastical building and of work otlrside the towns, e.g. castles. The Guild Masons were humbler folk. They were not allowed to build outside their particular city, but had a monopoly of all building inside that city, with one important and significant exception:-they were not allowed to build ecclesiastical buildings.

In return for their charter they had to maintain the fortifications. When a church had to be built the Freemasons were sent for, and apparently they called on the Guild Masons to help them with the rough work, e.g., to square the stones, etc. I suggest that Speculative Freemasonry is mainly descended from the Freemasons, whereas the few Operative Lodges that survive are probably descended from the Guild masons. This theory is borne out by the fact that while the Operatives have our g.s. they have not our s.ns, yet these s.ns are unquestionably old.

They would all have the same g. for convenience in proving to the Freemasons that they were really masons, but they would keep their s.ns to themselves, as did the Freemasons, since they did not want the other group to have access to their private meetings. Further, we find that the Master Masons of the Freemasons were entitled to maintenance as "gentlemen," clearly indicating that they were different from ordinary craftsmen (See Fort Newton).

After the Reformation no doubt Freemasons and Guild masons tended to amalgamate, and this explains much. Now if the Freemasons erected a lodge before they started to build a church or castle, we shall see that their meeting in the open would be merely occasional, e.g., while the temporary lodge was being built, and not a regular custom ; but the very fact that is was a temporary building, and open to approach by all and sundry who came to the site of the new edifice, is quite sufficient to explain why they had someone on guard.

Why, however, is he called a Tyler, instead of Sentinel, or some similar name? There are three explanations, and we can adopt which we please:-

1. To tile is to cover in; hence the Tyler is one who covers or conceals what is going on in the lodge. 2. In the old mediaeval Templar ceremony there were three sentinels; one inside the door, one outside, and one on the roof or tiles, who could see if anyone was approaching the building. It will be remembered that the old Templar Churches were round, so that a man perched on the roof was able to see in every direction. 3. That the tilers were inferior craftsmen as compared with the genuine Freemasons; poor brethren, as it were, and not admitted to full membership, although one or two were chosen to act as Outer Guards.

I am not greatly impressed with the latter theory, and my person predilection is in favour of No. 1 ; but there is a good deal to be said for No. 2. The tyler guarded the brethren from "cowans" or eavesdroppers. The former word is still used in the country districts of Lancashire and Westmorland for a dry-dyker, that is, a man who builds rough walls between the different fields, of rough, uncut, and unmortared stones.

When I was living in Yorkshire I had a number of fields so surrounded; the stones for which were picked from the hillside, and piled one upon another. No particular skill was needed to build such a wall; I repaired several myself. In other words, a "cowan" is one who pretends to be a mason because he works in stone, but is not one. Some fanciful derivations have been suggested from "Cohen," the Jewish priest. I disagree entirely with this view.

Why should the Jewish Cohens be more likely to pretend to be Freemasons than any other priests? As the other word is spelt as we spell ours, and means what I have stated, I see no reason to invent this suggestion regarding the Jewish priests, who were always few in number, and in the Middle Ages hardly existed:-the Jews were driven out of England by Edward I., and not re-admitted until the time of Cromwell. "Eavesdroppers" means men who listen under the eaves.

The eaves of a primitive or of a mediaeval cottage overhung a considerable distance beyond the walls, and between the roof and the wall was an open space. Through this space the smoke of the fire escaped; the general arrangement being very similar to that found in the tropics. The walls of such a cottage were often only five to six feet high, and thus a man could stand under the eaves in the shadow, hidden from the light of the sun or moon, and both see and hear what was going on inside, without those who were in the lodge knowing he was there.

But the Tyler was on guard outside the door of the Lodge; he was armed with a d..n s..d, and woe betide any eavesdropper he discovered, for our mediaeval brethren undoubtedly interpreted their obligations literally. Incidentally, I understand that nominally the duty of carrying out the pen. still rests on the shoulders of the Tyler.

With regard to the use of temporary buildings on or near the site of the edifice, it should be noted that during the building of Westminster Abbey there was at least one, if not two, such lodges, and they are mentioned in the records of the Abbey. One seems to have stood on the site of the subsequent nave. Thus we can see that it was essential that there should be an Outer Guard to keep off intruders, owing to the fact that Lodges were usually held in temporary buildings, often with overhanging eaves and an open space between the top of the walls and the beams which supported the roof.

The word "hele" should, in my opinion, be pronounced "heal," not "hale." The use of "hale" is due to the fact that in the 18th century the words "conceal," and "reveal," were pronounced "concale" and "revale." Since the words obviously were a jingle, I consider it is more correct to-day to pronounce it "heal." Moreover, the word "hele" means to cover over.

You still hear the phrase used, "to hele a cottage," or even a haystack, and the word "Hell" implies the place that is covered over, e.g., in the centre of the earth. "Hele" is connected with "heal"-to cover up, or to close up, a wound-and the meaning therefore is tautalogical, viz, "to cover up the word." (The Masonic s -t")

The use of the pronunciation "Hale" is to-day most misleading, and is apt to cause a newly initiated Bro. to think he has to "hail" something, or "proclaim it aloud." The C. is taken in hand by the Tyler, who makes him sign

17

a form to the effect that he is free and of the full age of 21 years. Why "free?" Well, in mediaeval days he had to bind himself to serve as an apprentice for seven years.

Unless he was a free man, his owner might come along and take him away, before he had completed his apprenticeship and, worse still, might extort from him such secrets as he had learnt from the masons. Thus the master might be enabled to set himself up as a free lance, not under the control of the fraternity. The twenty-one years is, I believe, an 18th century Speculative innovation, aiming at a similar object.

I think there is no doubt that usually in the Middle Ages an apprentice was a boy, who placed himself under the control of a Master with his parents' consent. The Master was henceforth in loco parentis. In the 18th century without some such safeguard (as 21 years) some precocious youth might have joined the fraternity without his father's consent.

The father might have been one who disapproved of F.M., and in such a case would probably have not hesitated to exercise his parental authority in the drastic manner at that time in vogue, and so exhort the secrets, which he could then have "exposed." To-day it is still a very reasonable clause, for it presupposes that man has reached years of discretion and knows what he is about.

Any real hardship is removed by the fact the G.L. has power to dispense, which power it constantly uses in the case of the University Lodges at Oxford and Cambridge. I myself was one of those who thus benefited. It is, I believe, still the custom in England that a Lewis, the son of a mason, may be admitted at 18, though the right is seldom claimed; but in some countries, I understand, it is a privilege highly valued, and regularly used by those entitled to it.

In masonry a lewis is a cramp of metal, by which one stone is fastened to another. It is usually some form of a cross, and a whole chapter could be written on its significance, but this casual reference must suffice.

CHAPTER III.

PREPARATION.

The next thing that happens is that the C. is prepared by the Tyler. This is a very important matter. There seems little doubt that originally candidates were str..d n..d, and even to-day in the U.S.A. C's are left in their sh-s only. In Burma we changed out of everything into a one-piece pyjama suit, a most convenient arrangement.

What we now have is a system by which the parts which have to be b. are made b. We take our ob. on our L.K., therefore that.K. must be B.. Why? So that our flesh may be in contact with Mother Earth. It is possible that there was a practical as well as a symbolical meaning in this , and also in the case of our deprivation of m..s. In some of the ancient mysteries it has been suggested that a charge of electricity was passed through the C. as he knelt at the altar, either from a battery, or by what is now called magnetism.

If any question the use of electricity in those days, I would point out that certain statements of Herodotus, to the effect that the Egyptian priests brought down lightning by means of rods, can best be explained by admitting that they had some rudimentary knowledge of electricity. The b.b. is in order that the S.I. can be applied.

The Scotch ritual, however, says it is to show your sex, but I am inclined to think this is a modern gloss. Personally, I should not regard this as conclusive proof in itself, for I have seen (when abroad) many well grown girls who had no breasts worth mentioning, while many native men had quite well developed busts.

It should always be remembered that this is the degree of birth and we were born n..d.. We are s. s. because we are about to tread on holy ground, just as in the East we wear slippers when entering a mosque. It is probable that the Scotch ritual has preserved a real tradition when it refers to the custom in Israel of removing a shoe, as a witness, when confirming an obligation.

Those interested will find the details in Ruth, where Boaz under-takes to marry Ruth. A.C.T. is placed about his n.. This piece of symbolism is old and world wide. On a vase found at Chama, in Mexico, several candidates are depicted going through a ceremony very similar, apparently, to a certain degree in M.,* One is being taught a certain sign, and the others wha stand waiting their turn all have C.T.s with a running noose about their necks.

In India this C.T. is the emblem of Yama, the God of Death, with which he snares the souls of men and drags them forth from their bodies. It is carried by - Shiva to indicate his destructive character in relation to human life. There are in masonry meanings within meanings, and I will therefore indicate a few of those associated with the C.T. , but I shall not do so with all the details upon which I shall touch. The C.T. is an emblem of Death.

It is fastened round the necks of captives as showing that they are at the absolute mercy of their conqueror. Thus the burghesses of Calais had to come before Edward III. in their shirts-note that-with c.T. 's round their necks. They were only saved by the desperate pleading of good Queen Philippa. But this is the degree of birth. Some come into the world with a caul which may strangle them if not removed, and in any case we are said to be born in original sin and therefore doomed to die.

*See "Freemasonry and the Gods" Birth, in the very nature of things, means death, and that is why the Hindoos have made Shiva, the Lord of Death, also the Lord of Birth. We ourselves are captives-souls bound by the chains of the flesh-and offenders against the Law of the King of Kings. Further, we come in bondage to sin, seeking to be freed from our bonds by the word of God.

The holding of the C.T. , and the dangers entailed, are sufficiently explained to need no further mention just now, though this does not imply there are not inner meanings. The h.w. is always found in every great initiatory rite. In general, it reminds us that as in the physical world we came out of darkness into light, so in the intellectual, and finally, in the spiritual world.

We come into masonry seeking the Light of God's word. In other language, to try and comprehend through the use of symbols what God really is. But as the veil of darkness is slightly lifted as we grow in years and our intellect awakens , so it is in the craft, and the first thing we see there is the V.S.L., itself a symbol of Divine inspiration; for without the Divine spark, which speaks from the inmost recesses of the soul, we shall remain in spiritual darkness all our natural life.

The C. is then brought to the door of the L. and challenged, but strange to say, in our ritual there is no p.w.. There was once, I have no doubt, and it is still in use in Scotland, Ireland and U.S.A. Moreover, it is one of the tests there when visiting, and if a man cannot give it he will run a serious risk of being refused admission. Strange to say, we do get it inside the Lodge, though perhaps most brethren do not realise it.

It is "The T. of G.R." (sometimes it is "Free and of G.R.," though this is less usual). But before entering we are deprived of M.. Now, among the Dervishes M. = mineral substances, but we interpret it M . . . I. It is M . . . Is!-that is important. "Valuables" is a real, but subsidiary, meaning. Let us consider this carefully. There is an explanation of why it is done in the lecture,-now, alas, seldom read in Lodge-and also, of course, in the questions.

These lectures were the real instruction; on them were based the tracing board Iectures, which were pictorial summaries, on which were set certain questions. Now the lectures (which can be bought at any Masonic furnishers) tell us that at the building of the Temple no metallic implements were used. Why? Because metals came from below. They were the gifts of the Thonic Gods:-the Gods of the Underworld-useful, no doubt, but being gifts of the

Gods of the Underworld they were in their very nature evil, and abhorrent to the Gods of Light, whom the white races worshipped.

For this reason the Egyptians continued to use stone knives to open the corpse preparatory to embalming it, long after they used metal knives constantly. The holy dead must not be polluted with the gifts of the evil powers. If there is anything in the theory of an electric or magnetic discharge being made at the time when a metal point is applied to the n. I. b. at the ob. , this would also be a practical reason; the presence of metal might make such a charge dangerous.

But the first reason is no doubt the original one, and probably the only one. The idea that we bring nothing into this world is, of course, likewise obvious; but its full significance is lost in our ritual, although seen in the Irish. There a C. is deprived of metals in the first and in the second degrees. The significance of this will be realised by M.M.'s if they ponder awhile on the meaning of the S.W.'s P.W.- "How hardly shall a rich man enter the kingdom of Heaven." That worldly possessions hamper a man's spiritual progress is proclaimed by every religion in the world which can truly be called great.

The Buddhist monk and the mediaeval friar alike agree on this. Why p.w.s. at all? Here we wander into a strange field, no less than that of old world magic, I think. The C. enters an E. A. Lodge from the outside world. Prior to his entry this Lodge has been opened by a peculiar ceremony :- a ceremony which, in the technical language of magic and the occult, raises the vibrations of those present; thus they are , as it were , raised to a higher key, and force is generated.

Now those who have studied such matters know that a body of men who are all concentrating on a particular subject do generate a peculiar, subtle, but powerful force, which has not been accurately defined by science , but is loosely called magnetic. In the old days of phenomenal magic certain words, when uttered in the correct tone, were believed to be in consonance with this "power," like a tuning fork is to a violin.

Therefore we give this p.w. to the C. to raise him quickly to the same "power" as the Lodge. But I am afraid I may be getting rather deep for our younger readers. All I need say further is that such p.w.s are universal in the great mystery rites, ancient or modern, and it is not surprising, therefore, that in some rituals we find a P.W. leading to the I degree.

CHAPTER IV.

ADMISSION.

Now our C. enters and is received on a S.L.. This signifies many things, one idea lying within the other. It reminds us of the pain we, as distinct from our mothers , suffered when we entered this physical world. It is a test of our courage and obedience. Probably in olden days blood was drawn, as a sacrifice. The Can. comes seeking for knowledge; self-restraint and quiet confidence should mark his bearing.

In all primitive initiatory rites most painful tests are applied, and if the candidate does not bear them with courage he is rejected, and told that henceforth he is to dress as a woman and will be treated with contempt by the men of the tribe. We note that the instrument is a Latin cross, the age-old symbol of suffering, and this is the only place in the Lodge where the C. sees this cross, (e.g. when it is shown him later) though M.M. 's may realise that there does come a time when he treads the Way of the Cross of suffering.

The use of a Latin Cross as the S.I. is peculiarly significant, for it is associated with pain and the danger of death, and tells us, in symbolic language, that the way of life is the path of suffering, and begins with the threat of death and ends in death itself: but by this hard road we draw nearer to the object of our quest. Next the C. kneels while the blessing of H. is invoked.

This needs no explanation, for he is about to start on The Quest and needs Divine help. But the phrase, "Relying on such sure support, you may safely rise and follow your leader, . . . , for where the name of God is invoked we trust no danger can ensue" seems pointless in Emulation working, for the danger was at the door and is passed.

At Leeds, however, they have a working which is, they say, derived from the Old York ritual, and it does explain this passage. I saw this ceremony at Alfred 306, Leeds. The C. was brought in h-w and bidden to k . . l., and after the prayer, the W.M. said:- "Mr. Brown it is but fair to tell you of the perilous position in which you are now placed.

Before you stand one with a d.s. in his hand, pointed at your n. l.b. , and behind you one holds the end of the c.t. which is about your neck; in this position of difficulty and danger, in whom do you put your trust?" Answer:- "In God. " W.M.:-"Right glad am I to see your faith is so well founded; relying, etc." Here you see the C. is in danger. Next the C. is taken round with the Sun, for this is the road of life , and in all ancient religions on entering a temple a man had to follow this path.

In Burma to this day you are expected to pass round the pagoda in this manner. The words are:-"Brethren in the N.E.S. and W. will take notice. " It is clear therefore that emphasis is laid on the fact that the candidate is following the path of the Sun, for otherwise why not employ the more usual phrase, "North, South, East and West?"

Now the Swastika, which may be regarded as the "lost sign" in Freemasonry (+), indicates the path of the Sun and is the emblem of life, whereas the Suwastika is the emblem of the life beyond the grave, for, according to ancient symbolism and eschatology, the departed soul went through the underworld the reverse way, just as the Sun was supposed to do, e.g. W.S.E.N.

This then, is the road of the Spirits. Thus the candidate starts on the symbolic (+) First suggested by Wor. Bro. Sir John Cockburn. journey of life, and in some of the eighteenth century rituals there is evidence that the way was made hard and difficult, to symbolise the trials and tribulations we meet with in life , particularly if we strive to attain to the Light.

This lesson is still taught in certain foreign rituals. In "Freemasonry and the Ancient Gods" I have discussed the probability of the theory that the Swastika was once used in our Lodges to represent God, as it still is in the operative lodges, and have shown that a square-a-gamma *, the Greek "G," and therefore that the fourfold gamma represents the four letters of the Hebrew alphabet which denote the sacred name of God.

I refer again to this point later, and so will content myself with saying that in an operative lodge the Swastika if formed of four gallow-squares, one of which always rests on the open volume of the Bible, while the other three belong to the three Grand Master Masons, and are placed by them on the Bible before opening the Lodge, in such a way as to form a Swastika.

Thus even to-day in the manner of our progress round the L. we are reminded of that age-old symbol, which is found all over the world, *First suggested by Wor. Bro. Sir John Cockburn. representing Life and the Sun, the latter being itself an emblem for God. The C. is then told to step off with the l. f. f.. Why? Because the Preserver in ancient mythology is always depicted as trampling with his l. f. on the Serpent of Evil.

This is so, alike in ancient Egypt, in India and elsewhere. But some may ask "Why should Horus or Krishna plant his l. f. on the serpent of Evil?" Major Sanderson, who has spent many years in Nyasaland as Medical Officer of Health and has been initiated into several native rites, tells me that among many primitive races there is a superstition that when entering a shed where rice is stored one must enter r. f. first, "so as not to hurt the Spirit who rules over the rice store." The same idea prevails among these people wherever food is stored, and we here get an explanation of "l. f. f.".

When fighting against the Spirit of Evil you do desire to hurt him, and so reverse the superstition, and step off l. f. f.. This is Major Sanderson's view, and I consider it is probably the correct one. It may also be well to point out that our ceremonies have come in contact, at various periods, with many different religious beliefs, ana this fact explains why there are often several meanings attached to certain points in the ritual, all of which may be correct.

The great serpent, Apepi, in Egypt, represents the powers of spiritual evil, e.g. the Devil. But it also specifically refers to ignorance, as is shown in the

Indian legend in which Krishna tramples on the five-headed cobra. The five heads, moreover, also have a reference to our five senses, which in that allegory must be cleansed of every evil thought. Thus we may consider that the World is represented by the C.T. and H.W., and the brotherhood helps us to free ourselves from them.

The Flesh is represented by the f. r. s. , in which we "trample" on the Tau Cross, while the Devil is represented by the snake, of whose existence we are reminded by the warning to "step off with the l. f. f.". Strictly, the C. should enter the L. in the N. , not in the West. The North is the place of darkness, and at birth we come out of darkness into physical light, and so in the spiritual journey.

This is done at Leeds. Out of darkness, Light. But the Light shineth in the darkness and the candidate comprehends it not, for the darkness of gross materialism is upon him until he kneels before the emblem of the divine light, the V.S.L.. The C. is then challenged by the J.W. and the S.W.. The J.D. gives the pass word "Free and of G.R. ," and the Wardens acknowledge its potency and bid him enter (Note "enter,") as if he were outside a door on which he had knocked for admission.

This brings to our mind the three regular knocks. For reasons which cannot be stated here, but which I will deal with more fully later, I suggest that the E.A. knocks remind us that man is Body, Soul and Spirit, and as in this stage of ignorance the Body is as important as the other two, the three knocks are all of equal duration. Lest any misunderstand this, I would argue that in the process of creation the Spirit first comes from God, secondly, clothes itself with a Soul, and finally enters flesh.

Thus, the first knock represents the Spirit, seeking God whence it came, the second, the Soul, and the third, the Body. To understand the full meaning of this passing by the Wardens one needs to consider why the C. is being led round the L..

There are two reasons given- (I) To show that he is properly prepared. (2) To show that he is a fit and proper person to be made a mason. Being made a mason symbolises the birth of the Christ within, and before anyone can attain to this mystical re-birth he must have progressed some way along the road of evolution, have gained certain experiences, and learned certain lessons.

Think again of the P.W., F. and of G.R.! In the earlier stages man is bound in materialismearthly things satisfy, and he is ruled by his physical passions. The C. for masonry has begun to desire more than the material: he has felt the desire for spiritual growth and knowledge, and so has become "free. " This is recognised as he passes the J.W. , who represents the Material Nature. Next he approaches the S. W.- the representative of the Soul-and with the aid of the P.W. is again bidden to enter.

Notice, having passed the material stage, when the Body reigns supreme, the Soul immediately, takes control, and presents the C. to the W.M.-i.e. the Soul calls upon the Divine Spirit of God to give L. to the C. The reply is significant, but is almost incomprehensible unless one understands the symbolical journey which the C. has just taken, and one is apt to wonder why the questions which follow were not asked at the very beginning of the ceremony.

Really they are most important! They constitute the final testing of the C. before he is bidden to advance towards the E. to receive the L. , and enter on the pathway which begins with initiation and ends with God Himself. Also they "are very searching: the C. being required to declare solemnly that he comes seeking knowledge, not because others desire him to do so, nor yet for unworthy motives of personal gain, but because he is prompted from within by a genuine desire to help Humanity.

Then follows a hint that the journey upwards is by no means easy, and patience, perseverance, caution and courage are essential if we are to achieve our goal. The C. having replied satisfactorily, the S.W. is given permission to direct the guide to instruct him in the proper method of advancing towards the L. This is by three squares which symbolise, not only uprightness of life, but also the three letters of the Great Name, Yod, He, Vau; Male, Female, and Variable.

In other words, God the Father, Mother, and child; and the fourth square is on the Ped., which gives us the final He, or the complete name of Him we seek,- Jehovah, or J.H.V.H. But the letter HE (pronounced Hay) is female, and its female aspect is emphasised by the position of the sq. and c.s., which form a lozenge, itself a well known symbol for the Vesica Piscis, as all who study heraldry know ; for in heraldry a woman's arms are placed, not on a shield, as are a man's, but on a lozenge.

A great truth is here taught,-that each soul is part of the Divine whole and cannot be separated from the God we seek. The C. is only just about to emerge from the darkness of gross materialism, yet the God he seeks is within him. True He is so veiled that many do not realise His presence, just as hundreds of C's tread out the proper steps without ever realising their full significance, but those who rise above the material start on the path of return to God, and each stage that they pass as they progress along the path, reveals more fully His Nature and Being. Notice, the C. only treads three squares,- Yod, He, Vau; Male, Female, Variable; the fourth square needed to complete the whole is on the Ped.

This is particularly significant-never whilst in the flesh shall we be able fully to comprehend His nature. No finite mind can comprehend the Infinite Deity. It is only after we have left the first initiation long behind, and travelled far, that we can hope to obtain that transcendent knowledge which enables us to understand fully, the Nature and Being of Him Who is the beginning and end of all.

Again comes the reminder that Masonry is free ; entrance to the path can only be gained by those who hear the call from within. No-one is coerced;-even at this late stage the C. is given an opportunity to retire. Thus he is asked if he is willing to take a serious Ob., and on his agreeing to do so, the W.M. directs him to k. on his l. k. etc.

It should be noted that the l. side of an individual is usually said to be "Femine," and it is not surprising, therefore that in this, the first and femine degree, the C. is told to k. on his l. k.. Notice the exact position! On the l. k. keeping the r. f. in the f. of a s. Now when you k. on the l. k. you must of necessity form a sq. at that k. , and, if you try it, you will find that you cannot keep the r. f. in the form of a sq. without keeping the r. k. in the form of a sq. also; so once again we get three sq's, with the fourth on the Ped.

Thus we get another glimpse of the truth already hinted at, that each soul is part of the Divine whole, and cannot be separated from God. The C. is only just about to emerge from the darkness of ignorance , and yet he is instructed so to k. that by his very attitude, -i.e. by forming three sq.'s with his body (the fourth being on the Ped.) he shows symbolically that the God he seeks is within.

Possibly the C. is not conscious of His presence , any more than he realizes the significance of the steps by which he approached the Ped. , or of the posture he assumes as he k's thereat, yet verily God is with him, and within him, and, be the journey short or long, back to God he must return. Once a M. , ever a M. , there is no such thing as straying permanently from the path.

CHAPTER V.

THE OBLIGATION.

Why should there be any ob. ? In all the ancient mysteries an ob. was exacted, and for this reason: -The secret teachings given in these mysteries disclosed an inner meaning, often of a most exalted kind, unsuitable for the general public, who were lacking in education. In the ancient world the external religion, with its worship of many gods, suited the ordinary man in the street, who was incapable of comprehending more advanced spiritual truths.

It would have been dangerous, alike to the populace and to the preacher, to have shouted aloud such a doctrine as the essential unity of God, and still more fatal to have attempted to describe His Nature. The danger to the populace was that the preacher might have destroyed their belief in the religious system in which they had been reared, while failing to convert them properly to the new doctrine.

For the preacher, the fate of Socrates, and the failure of the so-called heretic King of Egypt-who tried to popularise the worship of the one God, under the symbol of the Atendisk, or disk of the Sun-are sufficient evidence of the risks which would be encountered. Moreover, these mysteries all purported to teach certain occult secrets, whose diffusion among vicious, or ignorant, men would have been dangerous. Even in the Middle Ages these dangers were still very real.

Any deviation from orthodoxy might have endangered the social fabric of the community, and such an attempt was certain to involve the advocate of new doctrines in a struggle with Church and State which could only have ended at the stake. Within an oath-bound Society men felt free to speculate and compare their personal standpoints, while to the outside world they continued to conform to orthodoxy.

The fate of the Templars must have been an ever present warning to the speculative mind, in the Middle Ages. In addition, there is little doubt that the building trades, like other Guilds, had important trade secrets, and wished to safeguard these from interlopers. A mediaeval Guild , on the one hand protected the interests of its members, while on the other it trained those members, and inspected and passed their wtirk; thus protecting the community from deliberate fraud or careless work.

Nor must it be forgotten that in a building bad work might involve actual danger to the users of that building. For all these reasons it was right and proper that no one who was not a member of the fraternity should be in possession of its trade secrets. The ob. is undoubtedly ancient, but its full significance is realised by few. The penalty is d. , and in the Middle Ages I do not doubt that it would have been enforced, though to-day it is purely symbolical.

Studying it carefully, we note in passing the word "hele," whose meaning has already been explained, -and also that every printed ritual in existence is a clear breach of our Ob. The strict interpretations of this clause is one of the reasons why we cannot expect to find any mediaeval rituals, although the fact that the bulk of the members in those days could not read or write would lessen the temptation to make them.

From a practical point of view, however, the essential object to-day is to prevent anyone who has not been regularly initiated from entering our Lodges and the printed rituals usually does this, for s. ns., w.s. and g.s. are missing and a careful cross-questioning would undoubtedly lead to the discovery of an imposter, even if he could produce a stolen G.L. certificate. In the altered conditions of the present era our secrecy is more of the nature of privacy, unlike that which prevails in a political secret society, which usually has revolutionary tendencies.

The old penalty has many striking points. It means that the culprit will be sl., and his b. b . . d. in unconsecrated ground. More than that, the ground can never be consecrated, and, according to the beliefs of the middle ages, and also of the 16th, 17th and 18th centuries, the soul of a man so buried could not rest in peace , but would wander up and down in misery till the Judgment Day.

Suicides, for a similar reason, were buried at the cross road, and to prevent their bodies being used by vampires a stake was driven through the middle of the body to keep it nailed down. (It should be noted than even in England the p . . . s vary in different localities). Thus the culprit is not only d. . . . d to d . . . h, but to be a wandering outcast spirit till the day when the Great Judge consigns it to Hell. It is not perhaps a very charitable, or Christian idea, but that is what is meant all the same.

The T. is removed so that he cannot s. on his own behalf at the Judgment Day. The more effective punishment is, of course , a later "gloss," inserted at a time when; owing to better police supervision, it would have been dangerous to the members of the Order to enforce the ancient py. To-day, in England, it is the only effective penalty, but in some foreign countries d. is still enforced under certain circumstances.

In such cases, however, the Lodges are usually strongly political and revolutionary in tendency. But with us it still remains an obvious symbolical meaning. Immediately after the Ob. the W.M. says, "Having been kept . . . ."etc. We have seen that the C. has already been asked several questions ; these have gradually led up to this, the greatest and most important! Now the climax is reached. It is as if the W.M. says, you have declared that you are here of your own free will, not for unworthy motives, but led by an earnest desire for knowledge.

Your humility and obedience have been tested, and you are therefore entitled to request the fulfilment of the greatest desire of your heart. The question put at this moment can be answered by no one but the C. , for it is meant to teach him that essential lesson that no appeal for L. is ever made in vain. His answer given, the w.M. says, "Then let . ." etc. Notice the word restored.

Mystical rebirth marks the beginning of our journey towards God the Light, of our ascent towards God, but it is a restoration,-a journey back to Him from Whom we came. Exactly the same procedure is followed in the initiatory rites of the Turkish Dervishes. Among them, however, the incident is followed by a beautiful exposition of the mystical meaning of Light.

It is the Divine Light, emblem of God Himself, and of Divine inspiration. It is, moreover, present, not only in the sacred writings, but in every true believer's heart. The light of the sun itself is but a faint similitude of the Divine Light of God's love, through which, and in which, we have our being. Though not expressed in our ritual , this act has the same inner meaning, as I have explained.

So to the C.L. is restored, and he sees, what? The V.S.L. , the S. and the C.s. The V.S.L. is in a place of honour, because without its divine standard and authority the S. and C.s. placed thereon would be practically meaningless. These latter form a lozenge, which as I have already said , is a well known symbol for the Vesica Piscis , which represents the female or preservative principle of the Deity, without which we could not exist for a single day, or hope to be preserved from the powers of darkness which threaten us upon our spiritual journey.

Thus the W.M. 's words teach the aspirant that we have a duty to God, ourselves, and our brother men. The C. is raised with the proper g. , but this is not explained at once. Rather his attention is directed to the three lesser lights, which we are told represent the Sun, Moon and the Master. As our Lodges are at present arranged the W.M. should point to the S. for the Sun, and to the W. for the Moon , but it must be admitted that the lesson to be derived from these three luminaries is not very clear.

Indeed, the Moon plays no real part in our mysteries, which are essentially solar in character, while the implied contrast between Sun, Moon and Master is in no way helpful. In reality the three lesser lights are the W.M. and his two wardens, with their respective candles, and these officers have a real symbolic meaning of great importance, which symbolic characters they maintain consistently throughout all three degrees.

My personal view is that it was to the lights on the pedestals, and their respective officers, that this phrase originally applied, and that the Sun and Moon are 18th century interpolations.

THE THREE PRINCIPAL OFFICERS In any case this makes a convenient place in which to consider the symbolic meaning of the three principle officers in a lodge. The W.M. represents the rising Sun, and in this sense he covers two distinct meanings: the first in connection with the nature of God, and the other with regard to the nature of man. And a similar dual character exists in the case of S.W. and J.W.

The W.M. represents God the Creator, He who calls the Lodge into being, He who created the World out of Chaos. In India this aspect of God, the Incomprehensible, has been individualised as Brahma, so that the devotee many be able to comprehend Him, at least in part. It is the Master who opens the Lodge, who calls it out of nothing. He sits in the East, the place of light; but though he opens, he does not close the lodge.

That is the work of another aspect of the Divine Being. In the nature of man the W.M. represents the Spirit, the Divine Spark within us, ever striving for the light, never truly separated from the divine source of its being. This dual aspect of the W.M. and his principal officers must be borne in mind, if we are to delve down into the inner, or esoteric, meaning of our wonderful rituals. The S.W. represents the Setting Sun, and hence the Destructive, or Transformative , aspects of the Deity.

Among the Hindoos this aspect is called Shiva. He shall one day close the Grand Lodge of this World, when time shall be swallowed up into Eternity. The S.W. closes the Lodge. As the Destroyer he reminds us that Death, the great leveller, will bring all men low, and his symbol is the Level. This in itself reminds us of the caste mark of Shiva, which consists of horizontal lines. But in the nature of Man he represents the Soul, which alone enables the Spirit to raise the body towards divine things.

Without the medium of the Soul, the Spirit would be unable to influence the body. It is for this reason that the C. is invested in craft masonry by the S.W. or Soul, and not by the W.M. , representing the Divine Spark. Thus we learn that we must raise ourselves , step by step , towards the Divine Light. Shiva is, above all, the great M.M..

The J.W. represents the Sun in its Meridian. He stands for the Way of Life, the balance between birth and death. His is the sunny side of life. He calls us from labour to refreshment and from refreshment to labour. In the divine aspect he represents the Preserver, called Vishnu in India, of whom it is stated that as Rama he sent the skilful craftsmen , Hanuman , to build the bridge for Him , by means of which He crossed the straits to fight against the powers of evil in ancient Ceylon.

Vishnu is associated with the element of water and with corn, and his caste mark is a perpendicular, straight line , referring to the rain which falls from heaven. This symbol is remembered in our lodges by the plumb rule. In the nature of man he stands for the body, which perishes. He is H.A.B. in the Grand Lodge at Jerusalem. He represents the life and sufferings of the body, only terminated by death; the body which in every man dies before its divine work is accomplished.

Our divine temple is not finished at death: all that we can hope is that the foundations have been well and truly laid. In short, in this life we cannot hope to "see God face to face," nor, being finite, can we truly comprehend the Infinite , but we can hope to make such progress that, when called hence, we shall be able to continue , and complete , the work of our own salvation on the foundations of a good and spiritual earthly life.

Finally, it will be noted that in every degree these three officers co-operate to advance the C., and so it is in the spiritual life, for body, soul and spirit' must co-operate if real progress is to be attained. Next the C. is informed of the three great dangers-note the triplicity again-and the few sentences devoted to them must be considered in the light of what has already been written by me on the S.I., the C.T., and the Ob..

At the door of the L. the C. was in great danger, because entrance thereat marked the beginning of the ceremony of initiation into m., and initiation symbolises the mystical re-birth, the end of the descent into matter and the beginning of the ascent to God, and there can be no more critical time than that. The S.I. warns us of the dangers of rushing unprepared into the field of occultism, while the C.T. indicates the danger that the Divine Spark may be quenched, strangled by materialism, if we do not continue steadfastly.

But even when these dangers are passed, throughout the whole of our mystic journey there remains that last danger of our ob., namely, that of infidelity to the vows which marked our entrance, or of abandoning our further quest for light;-knowing the right, but deliberately choosing the wrong. This means death; not primarily physical death, but that greater death, referred to by our Hindoo Brethren as "Being born again at the bottom of the ladder of evolution up which we have for so long been ascending. " We next come to the moment, so long expected, when the s. . . . s are disclosed.

No doubt many Brethren could not suppress a slight feeling of disappointment at their comparative insignificance. Was such a tremendous Ob. necessary to safeguard a S. , W. , and G. which appear to be Purely arbitrary? This question is a fair one, and the answer is that the Ob. safeguards, not so much the G., etc., which are but the outward and visible signs, as the inner esoteric meaning, hidden in our ritual, and never properly explained.

Firstly, the W.M. instructs the C. in the f. r. s., which on investigation proves to be the tau cross. The tau cross was originally the phallus, and has many inner meanings. It is the emblem of generation and creation, but since these powers may be prostituted they must be brought under control. As the f. r. s. , it represents our natural and animal passions, which must be trampled underfoot and brought under complete control, otherwise we cannot make any advancement in Freemasonry.

In plain language , unless we bring our passions into complete subjection, we cannot hope to advance towards a true knowledge of God. For that, I consider, is the real search, or quest, in Freemasonry. Therefore in every one of the Craft degrees we trample on the tau cross. It will be remembered that one of the charges against the Templars, in 1307, was that they trampled on the cross, and this charge seems to be correct.

Yet these same men adored the Cross three times a year in their ceremonies and, moreover, fought and died for it on many a corpse-strewn

31

field in Palestine. I have no doubt this act of theirs was a symbolic one , associated more with the cross as an emblem of our passions than with the Christian cross of suffering. Yet symbols emerge by imperceptible degrees into each other, and so it is that we can truly say that Christ was crucified on the Cross of our passions.

In mediaeval pictures you will usually find that while Christ hangs on a Latin, or fourarmed cross , the two thieves are hung on Tau , or three-armed crosses. This indicates that they died for their own sins, but Christ, Who hangs on the cross of sacrifice , died for the sins of others. Thus, my brothers, the f. r. s. is full of inner meaning nor is this the only place in which we meet with the tau cross in the craft. Its higher and holier aspect when associated with the W.M. I shall discuss later.

CHAPTER VI.

CONCLUSION OF THE CEREMONY.

Having taken the f. r. s. the C. is given the S.. This he is told refers to the P. of his Ob., and no doubt it does, but it also seems to refer to something much more startling. The part of the body indicated has always been regarded as an important occult centre. In some strange way, the laws of which are but little understood, it has always been associated with the phenomena known amongst psychic students as Materialisations.

As, however, this subject lies somewhat outside our theme, we will discuss the point no further. But all our P. 's have a striking analogy to the legend of the creation of man as given by the Hindoo sages. From Brahma sprang all four castes. From His head came the Brahmins, from His Breasts the Kshatra, or fighting caste, from His Belly, the peasants, and from His feet, the Sudras.

The latter were not true Arians, and were not twice born men; in other words, only the first three castes were regarded as really and truly admissible to the Temple of the High Gods, and free to participate in Their worship. It will be noted that in this degree the S..n suggests the cutting off of the first caste from those below. This S..n, Bro. Major Sanderson suggests, was originally a mantra, or magic prayer, which must be most carefully guarded from the profane.

The T. appears to be an arbitrary one, although it may possibly refer to a certain piller. Explanations of this, together with the meaning, derivation , and significance of the W. , are reserved for the next volume, for reasons which will be obvious to those entitled to know them. No doubt, however, the basic idea of both pillar and word is phallic, and other interpretations have evolved later.

Having received s. w. and t. , the C. is warned to be cautious and told how to receive a challenge, then, having been given strength to help him on his way, he is sent forth in order that the important lesson of caution may be implanted in his mind. The testing by J.W. and S.W. are obviously of practical use, but I think that here also there is an inner meaning. The Body and Soul test the Cand. to see that the lessons have been well and truly learnt; also there seems to be a definite astrological reference.

Having satisfied these important officers, the s.w. asks for some special mark of favour. That is, the Soul calls on the Spirit, but is told that it is the Soul which must invest the regenerate man with the outward signs of the change he has undergone. This point has already been mentioned, but its deep significance must not be forgotten. It may truly be said that it is the S.W. who sets the seal on the candidate's initiation, and proclaims him as at length a member of the Order.

The address of the S.W. and the subsequent one by the Master, are fairly self-explanatory. But one or two points deserve stressing. The reference to the antiquity of the apron refers mainly, of course, to its use among the Operatives, and implies the dignity of honest labour. The present form of our apron is comparatively modern, but there is evidence that our predecessors, the Comacine Masons , wore aprons when they met in Lodge , and aprons have had a special significance among many religious systems.

Thus some of the Chinese gods wear aprons , and I have a photograph of one (See The Hung Society, Vol. III., op. p. 122) and this "God" is making a certain high degree sign. Among the ancient races of America the apron was also evidently used with a religious significance (see picture of the Toltec Preserver in "Freemasonry and the Ancient Gods"). The address of the W.M. lays stress on the importance of not entering the L. if a brother is at variance with another.

At first sight this may seem a somewhat unnecessary charge. Normal, well conducted gentlemen are not likely to start an unseemly wrangle in Lodge , even if they are at enmity; and should two men so far forget the common decencies of life as to do so, the W.M. has ample power to deal with the situation. The real significance of the injunction, however, is that it implies that the mere presence of two brethren who are at variance will disturb the harmonious atmosphere of the meeting.

This is a purely spiritual atmosphere, and the belief that such disturbance would occur without any open disagreement, is correct. In short, such differences disturb the spiritual atmosphere, prevent concentration, and can be detected by sensitive individuals. Every Lodge has an "atmosphere of its own," and any sensitive man who comes to it can detect it* I have myself noticed the different "atmospheres" of various lodges, and also variations in that of my own.

Too much regard therefore cannot be paid to this rule, and if ignored the Lodge will certainly suffer. The C. is placed in the N.E. corner of the Lodge for the reason given in the ritual, but it is important to remember that he himself is building his own temple-a spiritual temple to the glory of God. Why should the cornerstone be laid in the N.E.? This was for a very practical reason; namely, so that the Operatives could work round with the Sun, and thus obtain the maximum amount of light.

Symbolically, it refers, of course, to the journey of the soul, which begins in the N., enters life at the East, at birth, and so proceeds to the West, where death ends our day. The position in which the C. stands is not only a sq., the emblem of rectitude and of God, but at the particular point he make a "lewis," or angle clamp, which binds together the life which has been (in the North) and his future life (in the East).

In physical life the North is pre-natal, but in the spiritual it is before we turned to better things. Above all, such a clamp gives rigidity and strength to the corners, and assures stability. It will be noted that this position in like manner makes a "footing stone." The testing of the candidate is explained, but perhaps I ought once more to remind my reader that it is absolutely essential that we should leave behind us the baleful gifts of the underworld and the canker of wealth, which destroy spirituality. The lecture on the working tools explains itself. It appears to be mainly 18th century work.

CHAPTER VII.

THE CHARGE.

When the C. has been restored to his personal comfort he receives the charge. The first significant point is the phrase "Ancient, no doubt it is, as having subsisted from time immemorial." In "Freemasonry and the Ancient Gods" I have endeavoured to show that this phrase is literally true , and a stong claim can be made that modern Freemasonry is the lineal descendant of the Ancient Mysteries, via the Roman Colleges of Architects, the Comacine Masons, and the Mediaeval Freemasons.

The other significant phrase is that relating to "The Ancient Landmarks." Much learned discussion has taken place concerning what these are. Common sense indicates the following points as obviously falling within this heading, whereas many others may be matters of opinion, on which brethren are entitled to differ. I.-The signs, words and tokens. I

f these were changed it would shatter the universality of Freemasonry and prevent old masons recognising new ones, or members of various jurisdictions doin so. It must be acknowledged that the charge mad by the Ancients against the Moderns, that they had removed the Ancient Landmarks, was largely justified, for they appear to have transposed the w.s. in the first and second degrees. Still apparently, they did not entirely change them. 2 & 3.-Belief in God and a Future Life.

I these are removed, then the object and purpose of masonry is destroyed, since it is the "quest of knowledge of, and union with, God." Again, the elimination of the idea of a future life" woull destroy the teaching of one of the most important craft degrees. If these landmarks were removed, Freemasony would either perish, or else have to substitute a new object, as the Grand Orient of France has done. This having become atheistical, had to turn masonry into a secret political society, with disastrous results.

Hence it is that the Grand Lodge of England felt compelled to break off fraternal relations with that body. 4.-The Order of the Degrees. If these were reversed or changed it would reduce the whole system to nonsense. The remainder of this address is fairly clear as it stands. It contains excellent teaching, the meaning of which lies on the surface, and so we need spend no further space on it here. The first tracing board contains a great deal of useful instruction, but it is so seldom given in most lodges that we will pass it by, hoping at some future date to give it the attention it deserves.

The purpose of these tracing boards will be explained in the book dealing with the second degree, and we can therefore take leave of the Entered Apprentice. There is no pretence that we have exhausted the subject, much more could be written, but in a small book like this the author must restrict himself to giving an outline explanation, and suggestions for study, in the hope that his readers will follow the hints given, and discover further meanings for themselves.

CHAPTER VIII
THE CLOSING OF THE FIRST DEGREE.

The first degree closing is remarkably short, and its meaning is fairly clear. The candidate has not yet advanced sufficiently far to be able to appreciate any more esoteric teaching. He is therefore given one brief and tremendous lesson. The Destructive side of the Deity is invoked, and the same officer, it must be remembered, also represents the Soul. Thus, at the very beginning of his symbolical career, the novice is warned of the inevitable end.

During the ceremony of his initiation the fact has been impressed upon him that his spiritual advancement is by means of his soul, i.e. when the S.W. invests him with his apron. Now he is warned that the same soul which may help him to rise, may also cause his spiritual destruction. But even more this fact should show him that, when he has learned all that life can teach him, the Soul acting on the instructions of God, calls him to other fields of usefulness. It should also be noted that the S.W. closes in the name of the G.A., and by command of the W.M. , thus reminding us of Alpha and Omega, the Beginning and the End

CONCLUSION.

This then concludes our consideration of the meaning of the first degree. The author has not tried to be exhaustive , and would stress the point that usually he has only attempted to give one esoteric meaning, although often there are other inner meanings, each within the other. But he trusts he will have helped his brethren to perceive that there are indeed deep and invaluable meanings hidden within our ritual, and that his readers, having once started on this line of study , will not rest content until they themselves have discovered further inner meanings. If this be so, then this little book will not have been in vain.

THE FELLOWCRAFT'S HANDBOOK

by W.Bro. J.S.M. WARD

INTRODUCTION

By the Hon. Sir John A. Cockburn

In this little volume W. Bro. Ward justly emphasises the importance of the 2 degree. In former times it was no mere passing stage of a Mason's career. In the Fellowship of the Craft lay the whole body of Masonry. An Apprentice was regarded as a brother but not as a member of the Lodge; while a Master Mason was merely, as we still state in the ritual, an experienced Craftsman selected to preside over the Lodge in the capacity of Master.

The ceremony of Admission to the Fellowship of the Craft has been abbreviated and shorn of some of its characteristic features; for example a "Mark," which, placed on the stones wrought by a Craftsman, entitled him to his wages, is now no longer allotted to him. Nevertheless it is in the 2 degree that the essential elements of the Craft are revealed. The degree is founded on that symbol which is the basis of Masonry, and is regarded as the test of rectangularity in the material, as well as of rectitude in the moral, world. The candidate is now enlightened as to the meaning of the "Hieroglyphic bright which none but craftsmen eversaw." He learns that it represents the ineffable names of the G.G. as written in the four letters of the Hebrew Alphabet, to which attention was specially directed in the M. Ch.. It is as a craftsman that he becomes cognisant of the second P...r placed at the porchway of the Temple and he is taught that stability can only be attained by the significance of both p....... rs being conjoined. Herein is contained the Mystery not only of Masonry but of all the religions; viz., the Union of Heaven and Earth and the Mediation between God and man. As an Apprentice he has been taught to walk uprightly in the sight of God: his mind has become imbued with moral Principles: he now has to address himself to the much more difficult task of applying these principles in his everyday relationship with his fellows. The lesson of the J.W.'s plumb has now to be blended with that of the S.W.'s level. Spirit and Matter, theory and practice, with their innumerable analogies, have to be reconciled in solving the problems which are constantly encountered in life.

In the tables of the law one column contains the commandments relating to our duty to God, the other our duty to our fellow men. The Fatherhood of God involves as a corollary the Brotherhood of man. Therefore it is manifest that a stage in the progress of a Mason that lays stress on applied religion demands close attention. Although on the surface the ceremony of passing may appear less attractive than that which precedes and that which follows it, a close study will convince the reader that the 2 degree contains many lessons of priceless value which will well repay the labour of investigation.

J.A.C.

43

Those who have read the first volume of this series, which deals with the E.A. Degree, will realize that our ceremonies have a deep inner meaning and teach profound spiritual lessons seldom realised by the average Mason.

In the second voltune we are dealing with the degree of Life, in its broadest sense, just as in the first degree we were dealing with the degree of birth, and as life in reality is educational for the Soul, we are not surprised to find that throughout the whole degree the subject of education is more or less stressed. We should, however, realize that each of the degrees builds on the one which has gone before, and the ingenuity with which the lessons inculcated in the first degree are carried forward and developed in the succeeding degrees is one of the most striking characteristics of our Masonic ritual.

This is true not only of the obvious exoteric moral instruction conveyed in the ceremonies, but even more of the deep mystical and spiritual lessons which lie hidden bcneath the surface. For example, in the first degree we perceived that the st....s which led the initate to the Ped. when combined with that which we found thereon symbolically produced the Name of God, and in the second degree the main lesson is that the Brn. discover the name of God in the M. Ch., while the manner of approaching the Ped. gives us the Divine name, written with the five letters which denote that the Creator has become Messias, the King.

Thus among other lessons we learn that the second person of the Trinity comes forth from the first. When we come to the book which deals with the M.M. we shall pereive that that degree likewise builds on what has gone before. In the first few years of my Masonic career I utterly failed to realize the tremendous importance of the second degree, and used glibly to say that, while the first and third degrees impressed me greatly, and had valuable lessons to impart, the second disappointed me by its lack of depth and mystical teaching.

Many brethren have said practically the same thing to me, but I have come to the conclusion that those of us who think this are mistaken. The truth is that the real inner teaching of the second degree is less obvious than that of the first and third, but every whit as important, and until one has grasped its full significance one has no conception of the wonderful symmetry of our Craft rituals. In short, the interpretation of the second degree forms the key to the full interpretation of the third.

It is to impress this fact on my Brn. that I have written this book, and in particular have laid so much stress on the manner of approaching the M. Ch., and the full Kabalistic meaning of the Name there discovered. It must never be forgotten that while there are meanings within meanings in the Craft ritual, all of which are important, the great lesson of our system is the Mystic Quest after God, and the journey of the Soul towards union with its Creator.

With these brief words of introduction I venture to place in the hands of my Brn. this little volume, which, whilst not attempting to be exhaustive, will, I hope, be of some help to those who, amid the turmoil of mundane affairs, have little time to devote to an extensive study of the inner meaning of those ceremonies which they have nevertheless grown to love and venerate.

As one or two Brn. who have read this manuscript have asked me to refer them to a copy of the Kabala where they can themselves read what those ancient sages wrote concerning the descent of the letter "Shin," I would recommend the "Kabala Denuda," translated by Mathers, where they will find that, and many other points of peculiar interest to Masons. J.S.M. WARD.

CHAPTER I.

PREPARATION, P.W., AND OPENING CEREMONY

The questions which are put to the C. are really a test of the lectures, which to-day, unfortunately, are hardly ever given in open Lodge. The system as codified at the beginning of the 19th Century was really a most efficient method of educating the c., and had been carefully arranged so as to make sure that only when he was properly prepared should he come forward to be passed to the second. degree.

After having passed through the ceremony of initiation a summary of its main tenets, illustrated as it were on the blackboard, was given to him in the form of a lecture on the Tracing Board. The Tracing Boards were originally drawn in sand on the floor of the L., and therefore correspond closely with the pictures and diagrams used among primitive savages in the initiatory rites of a boy into manhood.

These primitive tracing boards are still drawn on the earth by means of specially prepared and consecrated flour, and are an essential part of the ceremony. To-day the masonic tracing board has degenerated into a somewhat crude painting on canvas stretched on a wooden frame, and its original purpose is therefore apt to be overlooked by the C.. This is peculiarly so in the case of the first degree tracing board, since the lecture on it is very seldom given.

In the second degree, as will be shown later, the tracing board still plays a very important part, and we shall have occasion presently to consider it in full, but the connection of the tracing board with the questions must be grasped- hence this short preamble. Under the old system, at the next meeting of the L. the W.M. went through the lecture proper. He asked the S.W. a sort of catechism, which the latter had to answer. This would take well over an hour, or, in other words, as long as the ceremony of initiation.

This catechism gave the exoteric meaning of most of the ceremony, together with a fair amount of traditional history of real interest. Undoubtedly much of it was allegorical, and although the bulk of it was 18th Century work, nevertheless it contained several very striking reminiscences of the Ancient Wisdom.

For example, the question " Whence come you ? " A.-" From the W." Q.-"Whither directing your feet?". A.-"To the E. in search of a M." Here we have something of deep symbolical meaning, and of peculiar significance in view of a slightly different, though cognate, phrase in a later degree. As, however, we are not attempting to interpret the meaning of these lectures in this book, we must pass the matter by, with the hope that our readers will make a point of obtaining a copy of them (purchasable at any Masonic furnishers) and study them at their leisure.

But the point which must be realised is that, while the tracing board is a summary of the first degree lecture, the questions asked of a C. are on that lecture itself. In short, the C. has to pass an oral examination, and the last question, namely, " These are the usual questions, I will put others, etc.," although to-day practically meaningless, had originally an excellent object.

It indicated that the C., and also the other members of the L., had heard the full lecture and that the former must be prepared to answer any question on it. In the North of England it is very usual, in addition to these questions, to ask the C. to repeat the whole of his O., and if he is unable to do so his passing is deferred until he can. Turning to the questions themselves, it will be noticed that great stress is laid on the fact that the C. must be properly prepared.

It is probably little known to most brethren, but well worth bearing in mind, that the Ancient Kabalists had a secret interpretation of the Old Testament, and one of the keys was to read backwards the Proper Names contained in those books. Now, if the words dedicated to the first and second degrees are read backwards, instead of the official interpretation given, they produce the phrase " Being fortified by the pratice of every moral virtue, we are properly prepared."

The significance of this in relation to what has gone before, and also to what will follow, is self-evident. The inner meaning of the manner of preparation having been given in the E.A.'s Handbook, it is unnecessary to write further on the subject, but of course if any of our readers have not seen that book they should certainly get it, as otherwise they will fail to understand the importance of these early questions. We now come to the question which is rigidy termed a paradox.

The explanation thereof, though ingenious, is obviously somewhat Jesuitical. The truth of the matter is that in Operative days lodges were held at mid-day, and probably on a Saturday, which has always been the time when the workmen receive their wages. The Speculatives, for their own convenience, changed the time to the evening, a fact which was resented by the old Operative members.

In the first quarter of the 18th Century, at York, Operative Lodges continued to meet at mid-day, while the Speculatives met in the evening. To-day, with the disappearance of the Operatives, a Bro. may well wonder why this untrue statement is still left in the ritual. The fact that it is there warns the careful student that some deep symbolical meaning must be attached to the time.

The full significance of the phrase is only revealed towards the end of a Brother's symbolical career in the Craft, and a detailed discussion must therefore be postponed to another book, but it is permissible to point out the following facts :-The sun is at its full strength at Noon; in his open pomp and glory; vested, as it were, with his full regal powers.

What more suitable time then for a solar cult to hold its meetings? And we must remember that Freemasonry is distinctly solar in its symbolism. Again, we were told that the J.W. marks the Sun at its meridian, and we have seen that this officer represents the body, hence our meetings are held while the body is at its full strength, and in possession of all its faculties.

Thus it is peculiarly significant that this question is put to the C. in the first degree, which degree deals with the "Natural" man. If the "Natural" man cannot protect himself at high noon against possible dangers, he is certainly helpless at any other hour of the day. We may therefore say that one meaning of this phrase is that the c. enters Freemasonry at the time of his greatest strength and physical well being.

That this is not a fanciful interpretation is proved by the insistence that a C. must be perfect in all his parts. In the old days no man who was blind, maimed, halt, etc., could be made a Mason, and in Scotland a Master of a L. still has to take an Ob. not to admit such a man. The reasons for this are both practical and symbolical. As an Operative Society Masonry was like a modern benefit society and had to maintain sick Brn. and the widows of those who had died.

It is obvious therefore, that they were justified in refusing to admit a man, not yet a Mason, who might easily become a burden to the society. Also, symbolically, every Mason is a sacrifice, and the Old Jewish regulations laid down explicitly that the ram offered for sacrifice must be without blemish, and perfect. These points must suffice for the moment, except that it is well to bear in mind that Christ was hung on the Cross at 12 noon, and our readers would be well advised to ponder over that fact and correlate it with Masonic tradition.

The next question and answer have misled many thoughtful Bm. as to the true meaning of Freemasonry. It should be remembered that it is addressed to an E.A., who as yet has had hardly any indication what Masonry is anything else than a system of morality. The first degree, for the most part, aims at teaching its members simply to be good men and true, and strictly to obey the moral law, but subsequent degrees teach much more than this.

Until a man has grapsed these elementary lessons it is not only useless, but dangerous, to try to develop his intellectual facilities, which is the main exoteric purpose of the second degree. For a Mason who has taken his third degree to give this answer as an explanation of what Freemasonry is shows that he has failed to grasp the inner meaning of even the second degree, much less of the third.

In short, this explanation by itself is only true when restricted to the first degree, for Freemasonry is much more than a mere system of morality, whilst even in the first degree the veil is very thin. The Grand Principles, in modern language, may be interpreted as true comradeship, charoty, and the search after truth, the latter phrase being better explained by the term the Mystic Quest after God.

The remaining questions are of a practical nature except that the phrase P.......t P.s. of my E. is often somewhat of a mystery to the newly made Bro.. Two interpretations of this phrase are sometimes given. Firstly, that it refers to the S....p, which is a tau cross, and means that we will trample under foot our animal passions. This is the manner in which we enter the L. when once it is properly opened.

But from the point of view of the C. it cannot refer to this, for at his initiation he did not know the S ... p, and so the other interpretation is the only one possible, namely, " of, at and on." This is interpreted as meaning that the C. entered F.M. of his own f.w. and ac., at the door of the L., on the pt. of a S.I. . (See lecture). Having satisfactorily answered these questions the C. is led to the W.M., representing the Spirit or Wisdom, and receives from him a P.W., which will enable him to enter the L. when it has been raised to the higher degree.

We have already in our first book explained briefly why P.Ws are necessary, but we will repeat our explanation for the convenience of any who have not yet read that book. They are a relic of old world magic. The C. goes out from a L. in the first degree and re-enters it in the second degree. In his absence the L. is raised by a ceremony which, in the technical language of magic and the occult, "raises the vibrations " of those present to a higher key, and in consequence force is generated.

Those who have studied such matters know that a body of men who are all concentrating on a particular subject do generate a peculiar, subtle, but powerful force, which has not been actually defined by science but is loosely called magnetic.

In the old days of phenomenal magic certain words, when uttered in the correct tone, were believed to be in consonance with this "Power," like a tuning fork is to a violin. Therefore we give a P.W. to the C. to raise him quickly to the same "Power," as the L.. Such P.W.s were usual in all great mystery rites, ancient or modern, and it is therefore not surprising to find them in Masonry.

It is worth noting that the Ancients were right when they charged the so-called Moderns, in the 18th Century, with having altered the W.s and P.W.s. As a matter of fact they reversed them, and the W. now given to an E.A. was originally given to an F.C., and vice versa, and the same fate befell the P.W.s. Those foreign Gr. Lodges who derive from England before about 1745 (for example, the French and the Dutch), still have the W.s and P.W.s in the old order, and in South Africa E.A.s and F.C.s of the Dutch Lodges are for this reason forbidden to visit the English Lodges until they have been made M.M.s.

The interpretation of this P.W. will be given at a later point in the book; all we need do now is to stress the fact that, as it is represented in our L. by C. and W., it is clearly associated with the J.W.. In the last book I pointed out that the J.W. represents in man, the body. This therefore indicates that to the spiritually minded man the simplest necessities of life are plenty.

All he requires, as the Buddha taught, is sufficient to keep his body in health, whereas luxuries clog the soul and retard its upward progress. I also pointed out in the last book that the J.W. represents God the Preserver, whose emblems in India, Mexico, etc., are C. and W.. From the anthropological point of view, it is worth remembering that among primitive peoples God the Preserver is also the God of Vegetation and the Rain God. He Who makes the corn to grow and provides food for his worshippers.

Thus we perceive that Freemasonry is perfectly logical in its use of this W.. Another fact of interest is that Quetzacoatl, the Mexican Preserver, wears E.s. of C. in his hair when he is wounded by the giant of evil near to a F. of W., and at that very instant makes the S. of a F.C. . The C. then departs to be prepared, and in the interval the L. is raised to the second degree. We will, however, consider the manner of his preparation before going on to the raising of the L. This varies in several details.

Most English workings are the same, but the Scotch and Irish have certain variations which are worthy of mention. According to the Scotch rituals he brings into the L. a sq. supported in his L.H., but, as with us, the I.G. presents the angle of a S. to his N.B., although to the Rt. B. instead of to the L.B. In the Irish Lodges the same B. is made b. as with us, but he is still divested of all M.s as he was in the first degree, and a C.T. is wound twice around his neck.

Thus it will be noted that everything save the B. is reversed. The Scotch, more logical, reverse even this. In American rituals the Irish arrangement of the C.T. in the second degree is also found. The reason for the deprivation of M's in the Irish ritual is because, as with us, the P.W.s have been reversed. This has a deep symbolical meaning, and is logically correct, but I must defer the explanation to the next book.

Reverting to the English method of preparation, we must realise that the R. side is the masculine side; it is also the stronger side. It therefore implies, firstly, that we symbolically have passed out of the control of the women of the household and have gone on, as it were, to school. In the first degree we were symbolically "Babes" or children, under the care of women. In the seoond degree we are youths sent to be educated at school, and the whole exoteric meaning of the second degree is the training of the intelligence.

This corresponds to a boy's training when he goes to a public school and is surrounded entirely by men. At home, under his mother's influence, he learnt only the simple lessons of morality; the lessons of the first degree. The second meaning, i.e. the stronger side, is stressed in the Scotch rituals, where the C. is afterwards told that he knelt on his r.k. to take his ob. because the F.C. ob..... is even more binding than the E.A.'s ob.

This latter fact is also accentuated by the nature of the P., but this we will deal with later. The C. is not H ..d, because clearly he is no longer in that state of absolute d.. .k.s which enshrouded him when he first entered Masonry. He has seen the L..t, and can never again return to the same darkness, although he may not as yet fully understand all that the Lt. means, and it is to teach him the true nature of that Lt., which is really the Lt. of God, that he takes his seoond degree. In view of what has been written concerning the preparation in the first degree, no further explanation is necessary.

THE OPENING OF THE SECOND DEGREE The W.M. asks the J.W., representing the body, whether he is a F.C., to which the J.W. replies that he is, indicating the test to be applied. Now, what does the Sq. mean in this case ? It is not, be it noted, the W.M.'s square or tau cross, but it is an emblem of rectitude of conduct. The right-angled square has always had this significance, and in many an Egyptian papyrus the Gods, when sitting in judgment on a soul, are depicted as seated on squares, implying that they are just judges.

So the J.W.'s answer implies that he must be proved by his moral conduct in the physical world. The F.C. degree indicates that the soul and body are now working in union, as is shown by the knocks, although, as yet, the purely spiritual faculties have little influence. So it naturally follows that in this stage of man's development we have a right to expect that he will conform to all the moral laws, and to the higher dictates of his nature.

For example, he should have a kindly and charitable disposition. If he has these, he is a fellow craft, but as yet we must not look for great spiritual insight. It is through his body that a man is able to perform the moral duties of his station. The S.W., or Soul, has little work to do at this stage, for it is through the body that we prove ourselves, and so it is the J.W. who is bidden to satisfy himself that all present are F.C.....

This being done, he confirms their testimony in his own person, and the fact that he literally is proved on the square must not be overlooked. It should be noted that it is no longer the Creative Aspect of God Whom we call on, but the Preservative. He Who places limitations on us for our preservation, for, unless we conform to the rules of the Great Geometrician we cannot hope to be preserved.

It should be remembered that by these ceremonies the Lodge has been raised to a higher plane of spirituality. Its spiritual and psychic vibrations are much higher, and to help the candidate to reach the same plane a P.W. has been given him.

CHAPTER II

PRELIMINARY STEPS

The Ty. gives the ks. of an E.A. for the Can., thereby emphasising the fact that it is an E.A., a stranger to a F.C. L., who seeks admission. The I.G. should therefore say, " There is an alarm," as is done in most old provincial workings, instead of "a report," a word suitable for announcing that there is a F.C. outside. Symbolically the difference between the ks. of an E.A. and an F.C. is most significant.

The three separate ks. indicate that the body, soul and spirit are all equal and at variance, whereas the one and twopence show that the two lower, namely, soul and body, are now united. This means that the soul of the F.C. dominates the body, and in view of the fact that spiritual progress while on earth is dependent on this, the arrangement of the knocks is most important.

The C., having been properly announced, is admitted on the S., implying that he has been proved to be a man of rectitude and has therefore learnt thoroughly the lesson of the first degree, which is good morals. Throughout the whole of this degree stress is laid on the fact that only a man of good moral standing can be permitted to extend his researches into the intellectual spheres.

The other important point which is early impressed on the C. is the fact that God is called by a new title. He is no longer spoken of as the G.A., but as the G.G. . We shall revert to this point later, but even at this early stage it is desirable to point out that the aspect of God emphasised in the first degree was the creative aspect (Brahmna of the Hindus), this is most appropriate for a degree dealing with birth, both physical and spiritual.

The second degree deals with the preservative side of God; it is essentially the degree of life, which is educational for the soul. After invoking a blessing the C. is led round the L. with the sun and tested.

Note, it is the body, or J.w., which now does the testing, but when C. is led round the second time, to show that he is properly prepared and in possession of the P.W. which will make him in tune with the rest of those present, it is the S.W., or Soul, which tests him. Moreover, the Soul first satisfies itself that the Body has done in work properly, therefore the C. advances with S. and Sn., before giving the P.W. Having satisfied himself on this point, the S.W. calls on the Divine Spirit, represented by the W.M., for help, but as in the former degree, is told that it is the Soul that must instruct the C. to advance towards God.

The Soul therefore tells the S.D., representing intelligence, to instruct the C. how to advance. This method of advancing is exceedingly interesting, and worthy of detailed consideration. The F. Sp.s undoubtedly have reference to the five senses, which represent the physical man, whilst their spiral nature recalls the P. within a C. hinted at in the tracing board of the first degree, and reminds us that round it the Brn. cannot err.

This clearly teaches us that we advance spiritually from within, by bringing under control all five senses and directing them towards that M.Ch. where dwells the Divine Spark, or God. As this subject will be treated at greater length when we come to the tracing board, we will merely point out that this manner of approach brings the C. to the V.S.L., which is God's revealed word.

It should also be compared with the manner of approach in the first degree, which in the last book we saw disclosed the fact that the God we sought was within us, while His triple nature, and likewise that of man, is subtly suggested. Here we are taught the same idea, but from a slightly different angle, and are reminded that we are approaching Him by means of our five Physical faculties. But as we arrive at the safe place we perceive

He is the same God, although during our ob. we learn of another aspect of His nature. One other fact is worthy of our attention. Whereas in the first degree the C. was instructed to advance towards the P., in this he is told to advance to the E.. What is the reason for this difference? It will be remembered that in the first degree he is H.W., and therefore unable to tell which is E. and which W.; by the time he reaches the second degree not only can he see, but his previous experience tells him exactly where it is he will take his ob..

Esoterically, in the first degree he had no clear idea where to go for light, he was merely groping blindly, although led by a friendly hand: but in the second degree, having learnt that the true light comes from the E., there is no reason why this phrase should not be employed. The position in which he takes his Ob. again makes the three S.s, but the instrument which he has to hold, and the manner in which he holds it, produce two more, making five in all-corresponding to the five senses, this irrespective of the sixth on the A. or Ped. .

To begin with, these five S.s indicate that all our senses must be dedicated to and ruled by, the strictest moral conduct e.g., "Speak no evil, see no evil" etc, but when we recollect that in the first degree we got by means of the Sq.s a suggestion of the Divine Name, we shall not be surprised to find that here again the Divine Name is indicated, but with two profound differences.

Firstly, the Name is complete within ourselves, that is, without needing to utilise the Sq. and secondly, it is no longer the four lettered Name of the Creator, Yod-He-Vau-He, but the five lettered Name of the Preserver, Yod-He-Shin-Vau-He, or Yeheshuhe, which we call Jesue or Jesus. As we learn from the Kabala, the Shin has descended to earth and by combining with the other four letters has made the Divine Name masculine instead of feminine, for Shin is masculine.

Secondly, it is the name of the Messiah. Now it has already been pointed out that the manner in which the Can. K.s, and also his preparation, emphasise the masculine aspect of this degree. Likewise the Name by which God is spoken of emphasises His Preservative character, in contra-distinction to the first degree where He is spoken of in His Creative aspect and the feminine side is stressed.

Finally, the fact that the whole Name is made by the man himself must be considered in conjunction with what has been said about the manner of advancing by the W.S. .c., and the M.Ch.. The Kabala teaches us that Messias is made flesh, and this implies more than the fact that on a certain historic occasion God became manifest in a human body.

It indicates rather that God is always being made manifest in every human being, and so the C., though he knows it not, is a manifestation of God on earth. Thus in a sense he himself represents the missing letter Shin, and so, when our ancient Brn. entered the M.Ch. to receive their wages and saw the Mystic name Yod-He-Vau-He, they themselves represented that fifth letter, which turned the name of the Creator into the name of the Preserver and Saviour of mankind. Perhaps I should point out this is not strictly orthodox Christianity, but Kabalism, although its similarity to much that is taught to us as Christians is dear.

Before leaving this subject I should like to remind any M.M.s who read this book of the manner in which they approach the Ped. in the next degree, for if correlated with what has gone before, the full significance of that manner of approach will be evident to them. The Sq. on the Ped. indicates that there is still another aspect of God about which as yet the Can. learns nothing, and its combination with the C.'s to make a lozenge should remind him that, though this degree is essentially, masculine, God the Preserver has also His feminine aspect.

The variation in the position of one of the points is explained at the time, but there is also a deeper meaning. One symbolical meaning of the Sq. is the material world, and therefore the body of man. In the first degree the body is dominant and over-shadows the spiritual side of the Cand.'s nature. In this degree the body is dominated by the soul, but as yet the spirit has not gained control over the latter.

The C....m. ..ses, representing the higher or more spiritual side of man, reveal this fact by disclosing one point only. The Ob. explains itsetf, and the Py. will be dealt with in the next chapter, as it can be more appropriately considered in conjunction with the Sn.s. As in the former degree, the Can. is r. with the proper g., which is subsequently explained to him.

CHAPTER III

THE S........TS

As before, the Cand. is taught by making the tau cross to trample under foot his animal passions, thereby reminding him that spiritual progress always entails increased moral rectitude. The first difference the Cand. notes is that the Sn. is of a threefold nature. This no doubt has a reference to the triple nature of man, but to the Cand. the most important fact is that whereas in the first degree the Sn. refers only to the Pen., in this degree two other lessons are taught him.

The first part is the Sn. of F., and implies not merely fidelity to his Ob., but obedience to the rules of the G.G.O.T.U. . We can only hope to be preserved if we conform to those rules laid down by Him for our preservation. The second part of the Sn., or H....g Sn., is said in our rituals to be the sign of P....y....r, or P....rs....e, but in its essence it is the sign of preservation, the sign associated with God the Preserver, under whatsoever name He is called, throughout the world.

In my former book, " Freemasonry and the Ancient Tools," I have adduced abundant evidence of this and here it is only necessary briefly to sununarise that evidence. In ancient Egypt it is associated with Horus; in India with Hanuman, the skilful craftsman who built the bridge of Rama, the seventh incarnation of Vishnu, the Preserver.

It was in this position that he brought the fruit of the tree of life to the dead and dying in the battle which Rama waged against Ravena, the Demon King. In Mexico, Quetzcoatl makes this sign when he is wounded by the evil giant. The Roman College of Architects at Pompeii painted it in a fresco depicting the preservation of OEdipus. The lineal descendants of the Roman Collegia, the Comacine Masons, in the 13th Century made a marble pulpit for the church of Ravello near Sorrento, not very far from the buried city of Pompeii.

This pulpit they adorned with mosaics depicting Jonah coming up alive out of the whale's mouth and as he does so he makes this Sn.-H..g Sn. and Sn. of F. complete. Now we are told that Jonah persevered in prayer for three days while he was in the belly of the whale, and was therefore preserved.

Furthermore, we must recollect that the early Christians, their mediaeval successors, and even the modern clergymen, have always regarded Jonah as the prototype of the Christ, for just as Jonah lay for three days in the belly of the whale and came forth alive, so Christ lay for three days in the tomb, and then rose from the dead. It is therefore not surprising to find that in England a 13th Century carving of the Holy Trinity at Peterborough depicts Christ making this Sn., for to us Christians Christ is the Preserver, since by His death we are saved.

Thus it will be seen, firstly, that the Sn. is of great and genuine antiquity, and has been passed down by a regular line of successors from the days of the Ancient Mysteries; and secondly, that it is clearly associated with God the Preserver and the idea of preservation. This fact emphatically shows that when we speak of the G.G.O.T.U. we are speaking of the Preservative aspect of God.

It is also worth noting that except in London and those parts of England where the influence of London workings has spread, the I.a. is always held in a line with the shoulder, and not at right angles. In the ancient representations of it both the London and the Provincial forms are shown-a fact of considerable interest.

Among the various initiation rites of the savages, as, for example, among the Yaos, in Nyasaland, this Sn. is also used with the inner meaning of preservation, and two p........rs form an integral part of their ceremonies. The P ... I Sn. is also old, for it is shown on numerous Egyptian frescoes and is referred to in the Book of the Dead. The significance of the Py. itself lies in the fact that among the ancient Egyptians the H..t was regarded as symbolising the good and bad in man.

It was weighed at the judgment against the feather, the symbol of truth, and if a man's life had been evil the H... t and the Feather failed to balance and he was rejected. If therefore the H..t could not be produced, clearly the man was doomed to destruction. This point should be compared with the T..e in the first degree, and just as in that degree the Thr. was indicated because it is an important occult centre, so here the H..t is considered to have a similar significance.

The part pressed in the G. has always been regarded by palmists as masculine, just as in the previous degree it was feminine. The meaning of the W. will be revealed in the chapter dealing with the tracing board, for obvious reasons, and those entitled to know will recognise where it occurs. As before, the Cand. is instructed how to give and accept challenges and then is sent round the L. to be tested by the officers, who represent the Body and Soul respectively.

This part of the procedure having been adequately dealt with in our first book, need not detain us now, for those parts which are peculiar to the second degree also arise in the tracing board. It is however worth noting that the phrase about the house standing firm for ever is not found in any passage of Scripture. It suggests the existence of an ancient masonic tradition, whose full history it is difficult to discover, but which is in closer analogy with certain phrases in the Book of the Dead associated with the Pillars, Tat and Tattu, which do convey the meaning thus indicated.

It therefore looks as if we have here a genuine old tradition, now disguised under a Biblical form, but not derived direct from the Bible. Once again the S.W., representing the Soul, calls on the Divine Spirit for some outward mark of his favour, and is told that he himself must invest with the distinguishing badge. To-day this badge has on it two rosettes, symbolising the rose, and made of light blue. Light blue was the colour of Isis, and later became the colour of the Virgin Mary.

The Rose is her emblem, and these two facts imply that all below the M's. chair are regarded as passive or feminine, whereas only those who have actually ruled the Craft, and represented the Creative Spirit, are masculine. Thus on the P.M.'s apron we get the Tau Cross, instead of the rosette, an emblem of the masculine and creative power. The shape of our modern apron is undoubtedly of comparatively recent date.

Our ancient Operative Brn. had large aprons, unadorned, and members of the different degrees were distinguished by the manner in which the apron was worn. Thus in the E.A. degree the triangular flap was worn with the point upwardthe triangle of course represents the spiritual, while the Sq. part of the apron represents the material. It was worn up to indicate that the spiritual had not yet entered into control of the material man.

It was usually turned down in the second degree, but, to distinguish bewteen the second and third degrees, one or other of the corners was turned up. The apron was suspended by strings round the waist, and these are still used on the aprons of the first and second degree, although in a M.M.'s apron these strings have been replaced by a band of webbing.

There are still aprons in the higher degrees however which are kept in place by cord and we shall consider the whole matter more fully when we come to discuss the M.M.'s apron, which is full of both historical and symbolical interest.

CHAPTER IV CONCLUSION OF THE CEREMONY

When the S.W. has completed his task of investing the new F.C., the W.M. further points out that the purpose of the degree is to indicate that a Bro. must polish his mind by a study of the liberal arts and sciences. This reminds us that whereas the E.A. is likened to the rough ashlar, which rests on the J.W.'s ped., the F.C. is likened to the perfect ashlar of the S.W..

The two ashlars are respectively therefore associated with the J.W. as representing the body, and the S.W. as representing the soul. Thus once again we are reminded that although the E.A., as indicated by the knocks, has not yet subordinated the body to the Soul, the F.C. degree teaches the important lesson that the soul must dominate the body, and that the intellectual faculties must be educated so that the F.C. may the better discharge his duties to his fellow-men, and appreciate the wonderful works of the Almighty.

In the few operative lodges which still survive the indenture papers of the E.A. are, of course, torn up on his being made a F.C.. Another important incident which takes place there is his formal testing to prove that he is a " square " man. This is done by passing a four-sided square, the four arms of which are extended, over his head and down to his feet, whilst to see that he is straight a five foot board, called the " straight edge," is placed against the front of his body.

The principal interest to us speculatives of this peculiarly shaped square is that by means of it half the secret masonic cypher was produced. The rest of the cypher was made up out of the St. Andrew's cross, used in the sixth degree of the operatives. After this brief admonition the Cand. is placed at the S.E. corner of the L. and instructed to stand in a position which forms a lewis, as in the former degree. (See E.A.'s Handbook).

Having explained the reason for this, which symbolically denotes that he is an adept, but not yet a master, the W.M. closes his brief peroration with the peculiar phrase " That as in the previous degree you made yourself acquainted with the principles of moral truth and virtue, you are now permitted to extend your researches into the hidden mysteries of nature and science." Now this is a very pregnant phrase and often puzzles the Brn..

Only a few minutes before the new F. C. is told by the W. M. that he is expected to do this. Now he is told that he is permitted to do it. So puzzling is this to many Brn., that in one London ritual at least, the word permitted has been changed to the word expected. This change, however, in my opinion, is a grave mistake, for the word permitted is there for a very special reason.

In the Ancient Mysteries it was believed that the masters of the higher grades held certain important secrets of nature, or, in plain English, had certain occult powers, such as second sight, hypnotism, and power to heal, and therefore, naturally, its reverse, the power to make men ill. To this day in India the higher Yogis claim the same powers.

They claim also the power to communicate with beings not of this world. Now the ancient Masters of Wisdom declared that if these powers were obtained by a man of low moral character, on the one hand his very life might be endangered, by his attempting to get into touch with possibly hostile spiritual forces, while on the other, he might use these powers for evil, and so become a danger to the community.

Therefore, only those who had given unmistakeable proof, through many years, that they were men of the most exalted moral character, were permitted to obtain that degree which entitled them to extend their researches into the hidden mysteries of occult science. Whether or not we to-day believe in such powers is a matter of personal opinion, although the hypnotic power is generally acknowkdged by men of science.

But even if we restrict the meaning of the phrase to modern scientific knowledge, we shall perceive that there is here a most important lesson. Every thinking man who has lived through the great war must realize that during it science has been used for the vilest, as well as for the best, purpose. Poison gas and the aeroplane which drops bombs on defenseless women and children are but two of many examples which makes us realise the dangers which threaten the human race if the hidden secrets of nature and science are discovered and used for evil purposes.

Indeed, it is not too much to say that if we continue to make further scientific discoveries, and use them irrespective of our duties to our fellow men, we may utterly destroy civilization. Therefore this word "permitted" conveys a most profound message. It warns us that knowledge without morality may be a curse, and not a blessing. Thus we can see that the ancient Masters of Wisdom were wise in their generation when they refused to permit a man to delve into the hidden mysteries of nature and science until he had given proofs that his morality was such that he could be safely entrusted with those secrets.

And so this little word permitted is one of the most important in the whole ceremony, and in no way conflicts with the earlier phrase that the Can. is expected. He is expectedto study these secrets, and is told why: it is because he has made himself acquainted with the principles of moral truth and virtue in the former degree, and it is assumed that being acquainted with them, and having passed the tests which qualify him for admission into the second degree, he will in the future act up to these principles.

The explanation of the working tools is 18th century work, apparently, and requires no further explanation, whether we take the short form usually given in Emulation working, or the longer explanation sometimes given in some of the Lodges. Perhaps, however, the word enthusiast used in this connection needs a little explanation. It meant in the 18th century language, a " bigot " or an extremist, just as the words zeal and zealot did.

In the course of years the exact meaning of many words in the English language alters, and some acquire a sinister meaning, while others become more kindly. To-day, the words " enthusiast " and " zealot " are generally used in commendation, whereas in the 18th century they were phrases of censure.

THE CHARGE The charge after passing is not given in Emulation working, but as it occurs in some other workings it is deserving of a short mention. For the most part it is ordinary 18th century work, without any very deep meaning, but we may point out that a craftsman is told plainly that though he may offer his opinion on such subjects as are introduced into the lecture-i.e., the lecture of the second degree, "now seldom given-he must only do so under the superintendence of an experienced master. In brief, he is not yet a fully qualified Freemason.

The other important point in the charge is the emphasis laid on the necessity for studying geometry. In operative days a sound knowledge of geomeky was important in the laying out of the ground plans, and a careful study of the ground plans of Glastonbury, and other great mediaeval churches, shows not only that geometry was of practical use, but that the main axial lines of the building were so drawn as to produce various geometrical figures of a symbolical nature.

Many of these were of a most complex kind, and would require elaborate drawings to explain their meaning, we will therefore only mention the constant use of the equilateral triangle-the emblem of the Trinity-its duplication to form the lozenge, the circle, and the elipse, or the vesica piscis. In general, Geometry symbolises the laws of the G.G.O.T.U., more especially those to be found in nature and science. Laws, be it remembered, which cannot be violated without jeopardising our moral and spiritual well-being, thus endangering our preservation, (or which purpose they exist.

CHAPTER V.

THE TRACING BOARD

The main teaching of the second degree is contained in the picture of the tracing board, and with regard to at any rate some of the incidents and facts an allegorical meaning is evident. The first important architectural feature mentioned is a pair of colunms, stated to have been set up at the porchway or entrance of the Temple.

These pillars seem always to have had a peculiar fascination for our masonic ancestors, and even in the early days of the Comacines we find them setting up B. and J. in the porch of the mediaeval church at Wurzburg, but their symbolical history runs back very much further even than the days of King Solomon's Temple. The two p..rs Tat and Tattu are found in the early papyri of the Book of the Dead in Egypt, and appear to have had the meaning of "in s." and " to e. firmly," but even in the primitive initiation rites of the Yaos, in Nyasaland, the boys, after various adventures, have to pass between two p....rs.

The original meaning of these p...rs was undoubtedly phallic, and in rites dealing with whence we come are obviously appropriate. The use of the word s. in a ceremony which, like these Yao rites, aims at increasing the procreative powers of the members of the tribe by a magical ritual, is obvious, but at a later date more ethical meanings were naturally grafted on to the basic one.

That this original idea was not forgotten when the twin colunms were set up by King Solomon is clear from the description of the chapiters. The net work, denoting union, combined with the my work, denoting virginity, and the subsequent references to the pomegranates with their abundant seeds, convey the same lesson, as do certain other adornments of the columns, but already other more evolved ideas had been grafted on to the age-old symbols.

Thus, the fact that they were formed hollow in order to serve as archives for Freemasonry, for therein were deposited, etc., seems to refer to the doctrine of re-incarnation. The constitutional rolls in this case are the effect of his past lives which are already latent in the child. At any rate it is clear that there must be an allegory here, for if intended to be accepted literally the statement is absurd.

No sensible person would really put the constitutional rolls inside a hollow p........r, they would be placed in the muniments room of the Temple. The reverence paid to p......rs or to monolithic stones is well known to every anthropologist and undoubtedly was Phallic in origin. In the Bible, for example we find constant denunciations by the prophets against the worship of stocks and stones; the stock being a pilar of wood corresponding to the stone monolith, to which the worshippers were in the habit of addressing prayers containing the phrase "Thou hast begotten me."

The use of the two p.......rs also renunds us of the gateway of birth through which we enter physical life, and so by analogy we get the idea that we must enter the mystical temple of Divine Life between similar p...rs. From such ideas would naturally evolve the suggestion that of the two p ....rs one was black, the other white; one of fire, the other of cloud.

Thus we get the opposition between light and darkness, day and night, good and evil, male and female. Moreover, we do know that in many of the ancient mysteries, and in the savage initiation rites of a boy into manhood, it was very usual for the Cand. to be obliged to pass between two p.....rs. The opposition between light and darkness is also taught by the checkered pavement of our lodge.

This pavement is a symbol used in many religions, and the Persian poet Omar Khayyam writes as follows:- " Life is a checker board of nights and days, Where Destiny with men for pieces plays, Hither and thither moves and mates and slays, And one by one back in the closet lays." Certainly this is one of the meanings of the mosaic pavement, although in addition, as Sir John Cockburn has pointed out, the word "mosaic" may be connected with the same root as the word Moses, which means, "Saved from the flood."

If this be so, the checkered pavement would be derived from the mosaic effect produced by the receding flood of the Nile as it left the land on either side dry after the floods. Let us now consider the names given to these two p... rs by the Jews. If we turn to the Hebrew words themselves we shall find that they had a secret inner meaning among the Kabalists.

These Jewish sages had a special and secret interpretation of the Old Testament, and one part of this secret was to read certain significant names backwards. If this be done in the case of the two words under consideration we find that their conjoint and full signification is, Being fortified by the pratice of every moral virtue we are now properly prepared to undergo that last and greatest trail.

The official interpretation given is not without significance as far as the first word is concerned, for God said that He would establish the House of David for ever, but while we can perceive the importance of the ancestor of K.S. what of the Assistant H.P.? Firstly, it must be recognised that the first column was considered to be the Royal colunm and the other the Priestly, and the explanation may refer to this.

In that case we obtain a declaration as to the necessity for Church and State as the foundation for civilization. It is interesting, however, to note that those who look for a Christian interpretation of our rituals are able to point out that whole the first name refers to the founder of the House of Jesse, the other name is that of the last male ancestor of Christ, namely the husband of St. Anne and the Father of the Virgin Mary.

Thus the names of these two p...rs represent the beginning and the end of the House of Jesse, from whom was drawn the body of the Saviour of Mankind. As there is a school of symbologists who consider that the whole of the Craft degrees can be interpreted in the Christian sense, these facts cannot be ignored. If their interpretation is correct the apparently casual reference to H.A.B., the son of a W., takes on a new significance in association with these p...rs.

In any case, in his progress through masonry this is the first mention that the Cand. hears of the famous Architect. H.A.B. is regarded as a prototype of the Great Master, and there does certainly seem to be a striking similarity between the chief incidents in the lives of both of them. But this fact will become more evident when the F.C. has taken his M.M. degree.

Before leaving the subject of these two p...rs it is of interest to point out that p...rs are regarded as emblems of stability among many races, and on a "chop," or certificate, used by one of the great Chinese secret societies the character KEH, meaning a p...r, is used, which among them has the further meaning of Stability.

Sir Johnm Cockburn recently pointed to a most pregnant fact. It is well-known that in the course of oral transmission foreign words become so corrupt in form that there comes a time when they cease to be intelligible, and in consequence attempts are made to replace them by a word whose meaning is known, and whose shape is similar to that of the corrupt word.

Many masonic students suspect that this has occurred in our ceremonies, and Sir John suggested that the Greek words Iacchus and Boue were the original names attached to these p...rs. Iacchus or Bacchus was the God of Youth and of the procreative powers, Who in some of the Grecian Mysteries was slain and rose again, while Boue means the primeval chaos, the dark womb of time, and so the womb.

This interpretation cannot be rejected lightly. Firstly, the appropriateness of such words to these two degrees is self-evident, but even more striking is the fact that the Supreme Council 33 degree of France gives to its members an esoteric interpretation of all the important words used in Freemasonry, and it interprets J. as the phallus, and B. as the womb.

Spiritually interpreted this would mean that the God of Life and Light, Iacchus, descended into the womb of chaos and brought forth Life. The tracing board having at considerable length, and in great detail, described these p...rs, goes on to give a certain amount of information about the men who actually built the Temple, and a very clear distinction is drawn between the reward received for their labours by E.A.s and that received by F.C.'s.

The E.A.'s, representing those who as yet are not very spiritually evolved, obtained merely simple maintenance, whereas it is specifically stated that the F.C.'s were paid their wages in specie, which, however, they could only receive in the Mid. Ch.. In other words, their wages were of a spiritual nature, suitable to their more evolved spiritualiiy, and that this was so is proved by the fact that they received them in the Mid. Ch., which is an allegory for the secret chamber of the Heart, where dwells the Divine Spark.

In all mystical language, and all descriptions of mystical experience, this hidden chamber of the Heart is spoken of as the place where dwells God in man. It is in reality a state of mystical experience, where the soul realizes, and for a brief moment of time becomes one with, the Divine Source of all. That this is so intended is clearly indicated by the statement that when our ancient Brn. entered the Md. Ch. their attention was peculiarly directed to certain Hebrew characters, usually depicted in our Lodges by the letter G., denoting God, the G.G.O.T.U..

Now the Hebrew characters stood for Yod-He-Vau-He, or Jehovah, the G.A.O.T.U., but since, as has already been explained, each F.C. in himself stands for Shin, in combination with himself he finds in the Mid. Ch. the name of the Messiah, Yeheshue, (Jesus) Who is the G.G.O.T.U., or God made Flesh, Who dwells among us. Bearing this fact in mind we shall the better understand the ceremony of closing, wherein the J.W., representing the Body, declares that in this degree they have discovered a S.S., representing God.

The fact that it is the J.W. who makes this announcement, and not the S.W.,is explained by the correct interpretation of the W.St. c .. se. This St..c..se is our own body, as we shall explain later. The ancient Brn. were not permitted to ascend this St...c...se until they had satisfied the J.W. that they were truly F.C.s, but he did not ask of them the F.C.'s W. as one might expect, but the P.W. leading to that degree.

This is of course right, for he deals with the simple necessities of life, which the E.A. receives, and which to the truly spiritual man, such as the F.C. claims to be, are plenty, whereas the true W., with its priestly meaning, belongs to the S.W. or Soul. The J.W.has no part or lot in that, but it is his task to see that the Body is in good condition, for a diseased body may easily hamper the Soul in its progress.

Masonry deprecates those foolish ascetics who torture and ill-treat the body, as much as it does gross and luxurious livers, who over indulge the physical and thus hinder the soul's advance. The explanation of the origin of the W., although taken from the Bible, no doubt has an inner meaning. In one version we are told that Jephtha, like Joseph, and before him Ishmael, was rejected by his relations and went out from his father's house to a strange country.

When, however, Gilead was threatened by the Ammonites and sent a deputation to him begging him to come to their help and organise armed resistance, he forgave the unkindness he had suffered and saved his native city. Thus we can see that, like One who came after him, he was " The stone which the Builders rejected," which became the headstone of the corner. So here again we get a reference to the Saviour of men and to Preservation.

The W. St.....c..se with its three, five, seven or more steps, must have puzzled many thoughtful Brn., who have no doubt wondered why it was that those who codified our rituals could not make up their minds concerning the exact number of steps the St..c...se had. This very fact warns us that it is an allegory, for the thing disguised under this name can be considered to consist of three parts, five parts, seven parts, and possibly more.

The three who rule a Lodge represent the Body, Soul, and Spirit which constitute Man. The five who form a Lodge are the five senses of the physical man. But the physical man has both soul and spirit, each of which has its own peculiar sense, the Soul having psychic faculties, and the Spirit mystical and inspirational. As the Bible indicates in the past there have been men who had second sight, and prophets who spoke by Divine inspiration.

Although while on earth the ordinary man only functions through the five physical senses, those who are approaching perfection, such as the great Masters and religious teachers of the world, function through all seven. The reference to the five noble orders of architecture is certainly an 18th century addition, for our mediaeval Brn. cared nothing about them, while the reference to the seven liberal arts and sciences is probably a post-reference gloss.

They are good enough for an exoteric interpretation, but obviously disguise something more profound. The five noble orders of architecture when applied to the Temple of K.S., are, of course, an absurd anachronism. Perhaps at this point one should explain that the Temple at Jerusalem, masonically, is an allegory for the Temple of Humanity raised to the glory of God, or, to use a Christian simile, the Church of Christ on earth, into whose fabric every true mason is built, dedicating his body and soul as a perfect ashlar in its construction.

This W. St....c..se spiralled round a central column, so that when the Brn. reached the top they had advanced neither to the East nor to the West, but were still revolving around the centre. To an Eastern Bro. this W.St c..se will certainly recall the ladder of re-incarnation, by the gradual ascent of which the Soul in time returns to God, from Whom it came, travelling upwards in a spiral.

But to the Western mind this St..c..se is our own body, subdued, brought under control, and dedicated to the glory of God. This done we receive our wages, which are knowledge of God in that hidden chamber which is within us. No other man and no external organisation can really give us knowledge of God, that is an experience which each must discover for himself, and in himself, as every mystic has taught, no matter to what external religion he conformed.

Mysticism is not an organised religion, in rivalry with any of the established faiths, but is the real truth enshrined in every religion, and the force which gives that religion vitality. Therefore it is that we find among Mahomedans, Buddhists, Jews, Hindus and Christians, men who while they often employ different symbols, use them to describe precisely the same spiritual experiences. Finally, let us note that the last guardian who has to be passed is the Soul, which itself passes the man who is a true F.C. into that hidden Ch..

When he has thus proved himself a true priest in the spiritual sense, the Soul enables him to discover the God Who is within him, and that this Divine Spark is ever linked to the Source of All. It should be clearly understood, however, that this discovery of God within ourselves is not the end of the Mystic Quest, for the evolving Soul has other experiences to go through, some of a most painful spiritual nature, before he achieves final and complete union with the Source of his being.

But until he has had this first experience, this first realisation of the Divine Spark within him, he cannot start on the real quest; for he is not yet properly prepared. He may, and will, come out from that secret Ch. again and again, to take his part in the ordinary life of the world, but having once glimpsed the splendour of the Divine he will realise the glorious heritage to which he is the heir and will not be content until he has completed his journey.

Nevertheless, it may truly be said that these occasional experiences, brief and passing though they be, are the just reward of his labours. This then is the great lesson of the second degree, that by ourselves, and in ourselves, we can discover and realize God, more especially in His Preservative aspect. This discovery means more than an acquiescence in the statement of others that there is such a Being as God, it is the realisation by oneself of this stupendous fact, a thing almost impossible to describe in words except to those who have experienced it, while to them it needs no description.

CHAPTER VI.

CLOSING CEREMONY

As in the first degree, the Spirit calls on the Body and Soul to show that they are on guard against this world. The Spirit then asks the body what it has discovered now that it has conformed to the laws of rectitude, as a true F.C., and the Body replies that it has discovered a S....d S....I. This S...d S...I, of course, is that same letter G mentioned in the tracing board, which corresponds with the Hebrew characters for the Name of God.

As we have already explained the full significance of these four letters we will not now discuss them further, but a few brief lines dealing with the valuable suggestion of Sir John Cockburn, that the letter G was originally depicted in the mediaeval lodge by a sq., calls for some consideration. Sir John has pointed out on many occasions that the sq., more particularly the gallows sq., was always regarded with very great veneration by the Masons, because not only was it an important working tool, with a symbolical meaning attached to it, but it was also the shape of the gamma, or G., in the Greek alphabet, as well as in the ecclesiastical script used in mediaeval Europe.

Thus the letter G and the gallows sq. were the same shape, and stood alike for God and His great characteristic, "Justice." Indeed, in mediaeval paintings the sq. is often found embroidered on the vestments of the disciples, and when depicted separately these are called "gammadias," that is "gammas," but when combined to form the Swastica it is called the "gammadion." As Sir John points out, references to this identification of the sq. and the G. are found in several old rituals.

For example:- Q.-Why did you get to be made an F.C.? A.-On account of the letter G.- Also an old Masonic legend found in one of these rituals, describing a murderous assault made on one of the chief overseers of the work by some of the workman, relates that one of the wretches struck the overseer a blow over the heart with a sq..

When the victim was subsequently discovered those who found him noticed a faint trace of the letter G on his breast, and they understood it as symbolising the whole-hearted devotion which the victim had always displayed towards God, the G.G.O.T.U. Another interesting point about the sq. is that if four right angles are joined together with the angles inward, an equal-armed cross, or cross of the cardinal points, is formed.

This cross, of course, has many inner meanings, but one at least is that it represents the earth and matter, just as does the four-sided sq., which also can be formed out of four gallows sq..s. Finally the Swastica which later symbolised the sun, is also composed of four right angles; hence the vital fluid permeating matter makes of it a living soul. In this last aspect the Swastica becomes an emblem for God Himself, and thus the sq. in itself represents not only God but also the universe, which He preserves by His Divine Spirit.

So it will be seen that the S....d S...I which the F.C.'s declare that they have discovered is of far greater significance than most brn. would suspect; in fact, in these few brief words of the closing ceremony we obtain a summary of the whole purpose of the degree, and realise why, throughout the whole of it, the sq. is emphasised.

Nor must we forget that when he announces this discovery the J.W. stands in the correct position to indicate that he represents that fifth letter, the missing " sh," which changes the name of the Creator into that of the Preserver-Yeheshue. Moreover, he declares the S...d S...I is situated in the C...e of the building. Bearing in mind that in the tracing board we were told that our ancient brn. discovered this symbol in the M...e Ch., we shall perceive that the Lodge itself is now the Ch., into which the Cand. has ascended by the W...g S...c...e of the f....St...s which led him to the E.

The fact that it is in the C...e reminds us of that hidden centre in every man, where resides the Divine Spark, and brings to our recollection the statement in the first tracing board that there is a point within a circle around which the Brn. cannot err. In lodge in the Provinces which have their own Temples, it is usual to see depicted on the roof a pentacle, in the middle of which can be seen the letter G.

In this case the pentacle represents man with his five senses, with the G at the cente to remind us of the Divine Spark within. On the floor directly underneath is inlaid in brass a point within a circle, which circle is bounded on the north and south side by two grand parallel lines, usually described as the two St. Johns, but stated in our ritual to represent Moses and K.S.. They also undoubtedly symbolize many other things, e.g., the two pillars of night and day, good and evil, male and female, etc.

The point I wish to stress, however, is that the brass point at the c. of the c. is directly underneath the G in the pentacle on the roof, thus emphasising the interpretation we have been studying. It is a thousand pities that in most of our London Lodges both these essential ornaments of the Lodge are omitted from the decorations, as by so doing their intimate connection is apt to be overlooked by the brn., and even the words of the ritual become untrue.

Thus the F.C. degree teaches us that we only begin to recognize the God within us when we have lived a good life. There is also, probably, a reference to the word "Generation," which is naturally associated with the life of the fully developed man. The meaning of this is that the power of begetting is a Godlike gift, for it creates physical life, and we must use it with respect and for the noblest ends.

It is only when we are masters of our passions in this respect that we are fitted for the last and greatest trial." It is noteworthy that it is the J.W., representing the Body, who plays the most important part in the closing of this degree, which is, of course, appropriate, as we have been dealing throughout with the body and its five senses.

This phase is carried through to the very end, as is shown in the curious doggerel lines with which the J.W. performs the last act of closing. As given in Emulation they are only three, but in the Provinces they are four, and form a curious jingling rhyme, which runs as follows:- Happy have we met, Happy have we been, Happy may we part, And happy meet again.

Personally I prefer this version to that in Emulation which, for some unaccountable reason, omits the second line, although it is quite as important as the first or third. Clearly the Brn. might be happy to part because they had been unhappy during the ceremony! The inner significance of the lines, however, is that the body bears testimony that earthly happiness can only be found by those who know God.

The closing prayer by the W.M. contains one important reference, which seems to be an ancient landmark carried down in our ritual from a long distant past, viz., the All-seeing Eye. This Sacred Eye was a divine emblem and an important talisman among the ancient Egyptians, even as it still is among the Chinese, who paint it on the bows of their ships to protect them and preserve them from misfortune.

It is essentially an emblem of God the Preserver, and its inclusion in the closing prayer of the second degree indicates how carefully the preservative aspect of God is stressed, from the beginning to the very end of the ceremony.

This concludes all that it is possible to deal with in this little book concerning the second degree, but those whose interest has been aroused will be well advised to do two things ; firstly to study the ritual itself, in order to discover additional inner meanings, which do exist, although they have not been dealt with here lest we should befog our newly passed Brn.; and secondly, study the lectures on this degree, which contain a great deal of interesting information, much of it with an inner meaning seldom appreciated by those who have only read them through hastily.

Finally we would add that in the M.M.'s Handbook will be found an explanation of several points which we have had to omit in this book, but which show how carefully each of our degrees is linked up with the one that follows, and how to the attentive student they gradually unfold many important and illuminating truths.

THE MASTER MASON'S HANDBOOK

by W.Bro. J.S.M. WARD

INTRODUCTION

By the Hon. Sir John A. Cockburn

W.Bro. Ward has lost no time in supplying his large circle of readers with this little book on the 3 degree. With becoming reverence he touches on the last great lesson which Masonry presents to the mind of the Craftsman. Among the manifold blessings that Freemasonry has conferred on mankind none is greater than that of taking the sting from death and robbing the grave of victory. No man can be called Free who lives in dread of the only event that is certain in his life. Until emancipated from the fear of death, he is all his life long subject to bondage. Yet how miserably weak is this phantom king of Terrors who enslaves so many of the uninitiated. As Francis Bacon remarked, there is no passion in the mind of man that does not master the dread of death. Revenge triumphs over it; love slights it; honour aspireth to it; grief flieth to it. Death has always been regarded as the elucidation of the Great Mystery. It was only at the promise of dissolution that the seeker after the Elixir of Life exclaimed Eureka. Masonry regards death but as the gate of life, and the Master Mason learns to look forward with firm but humble confidence to the moment when he will receive his summons to ascend to the Grand Lodge above.

Brother Ward very properly attaches much significance to the Pass Word leading to the 2 degree and 3 degree. In the Eleusinian Mysteries an ear of corn was presented to the Epoptai. This, as an emblem of Ceres, represented by the S.W., is appropriate to the F.C.'s, who are under the guidance of that officer, while the name of the first artificier in metals, which is reminiscent of Vulcan, the Celestial Blacksmith, seems specially befitting to the attributes of the J.W., as it was in the days before 1740. The author sees in the lozenge formed by two of the great lights a representation of the Vesica Piscis. This symbol, whose literal meaning is "the bladder of the fish,' is of deep significance. Some see in it the essential scheme of ecclesiastical architecture. But as the spiritually blind are unable to discern similitudes, so those who are gifted with deep insight are apt to over estimate analogies. The Vesica Piscis being, as Brother Ward rightly states, a feminine emblem, and therefore one sided, can hardly represent the equilibrium attained by the conjunction of the square and compasses. These respectively stand for the contrasted correlatives which pervade Creation, and, like the pillars, are typical when conjoined of new stability resulting from their due proportion in the various stages of Evolution. The progressive disclosures of the points of the compasses seems to indicate the ultimate realisation of the spirituality of matter; the at-one-ment and reconciliation at which Freemasonry and all true religions aim. Brother Ward repeatedly points out the similarity that exists between the lessons of Christianity and of Freemasonry. It is indeed difficult to distinguish between them, The Ancient Mysteries undoubtedly possessed in secret many of the truths proclaimed in the gospel. St. Augustine affirms that Christianity, although not previously known by that name, had always existed. But whereas the hope of immortality was formerly in the Mysteries confined to a favoured few, the new Covenant opened the Kingdom of Heaven to all believers. Incidentally this little volume clears up many passages which are obscure in the Ritual. For example, there could be no object in directing that the F.C's, who, on account of their trust-worthiness, were selected by the King to search for the Master, should be clothed in white to prove their innocence. That was already beyond question. The order was evidently meant for the repentant twelve who took no actual part in the crime. This and similar inconsistencies in the Ritual may be accepted as evidence of its antiquity. Had it been a modern compilation such contradictions would have been studiously avoided.

It is probable that many earnest Masons may not agree with all Brother Ward's interpretations. Nor can such unanimity reasonably be expected. Freemasonry, as a gradual accretion of the Wisdom of Ages Immemorial, bears traces of many successive schools of thought. But all its messages are fraught with hope for the regeneration of humanity. The author intimated his desire in this series of handbooks to lead others to prosecute the study of Masonry for themselves; and indeed he has abundantly proved that in its unfathomable depths there are many gems of priceless ray serene which will well repay the search. Brother Ward is heartily to be congratulated on having attained the object he had in view.

J.A.C.

PREFACE

THE third degree in Freemasonry is termed the Sublime Degree and the title is truly justified. Even in its exoteric aspect its simple, yet dramatic, power must leave a lasting impression on the mind of every Cand.. But its esoteric meaning contains some of the most profound spiritual instruction which it is possible to obain to-day.

Even the average man, who entered The Craft with little realisation of its real antiquity and with the solemnity of this, its greatest degree. In its directness and apparent simplicity rests its tremendous power. The exoteric and esoteric are interwoven in such a wonderful way that it is almost imopssible to separate the one from the other, and the longer it is studied the more we realise the profound and ancient wisdom concealed therein. Indeed, it is probable that we shall never master all that lies hidden in this degree till we in very truth pass through that reality of which it is a allegory.

The two degrees which have gone before, great and beautiful though they be are but the training and preparation for the message which the third degree holds in almost every line of the ritual. Here at length we learn the true purpose of Freemasonry. It is not merely a system of morality veiled in allegory and illustrated by symbols, but a great adventure, a search after that which was lost; in other words, the Mystic Quest, the craving of the Soul to comprehend the nature of God and to achieve union with Him.

Different men vary greatly; to some the most profound teachings appeal, while to others simpler and more direct instruction is all they crave. But there is hardly a man who has not, at some time or other, amid the turmoil and distraction of this material world, felt a strange and unaccountable longing for knowledge as to why he was ever sent here, whence he came, and whither he is wending. At such times he feels like a wanderer in a strange land, who has almost forgotten his native country, because he left it so long ago, but yet vaguely realises that he is an exile, and dimly craves for some message from that home which he knew of yore.

This is the voice of the Divine Spark in man calling out for union with the Source of its being, and at such times the third degree carries with it a message which till then, perhaps, the brother had not realized. The true s...ts are lost, but we are told how and where we shall find them. The gateway of d. opens the way to the p. within the c., where the longing spirit will find peace in the arms of the Father of All.

Thus it will be seen that the third degree strikes a more solemn note thane even that of d. itself, and I have endeavoured in this little book to convey in outline form some part at least of this sublime message.

As in my previous books, I freely confess that I have not covered the whole ground. Not only would it be impossible to do so in a book of this size, but in so doing I should have defeated one of my principal objects in writing namely, to inspire others to study for themselves and endeavour to find in our ceremonies further and deeper meanings.

The success of the earlier books shows clearly that my efforts have not been in vain, and that the brethren are more than anxious to fathom the inner meaning of the ceremonies we all love so well. This book completes the series dealing with the meaning of the three craft degrees, but their popularity has convinced me that the experiment of producing a small and inexpensive handbook has been completely justified. I have therefore been encouraged to write further volumes, and the next of the series will be an outline history of Freemasonry " from time Immemorial."

PREFACE TO SECOND EDITION

The success of the fust edition of this book has necessitated a second wherein I have corrected a few printing errors and added a few points which may help my brother students.

From the number of letters I have received from all parts of the world, thanking me for the light these books throw on the meaning of our ceremonies, it is clear that the new members who are entering our Order are tending to take an increasing interest in the meaning of our Rites and are no longer content to regard the Ceremonies merely as a pastime for an idle hour.

J.S.M. WARD.

CHAPTER I.

QUESTIONS AND P.W.

Those of our Brethren who have read the previous two books of this series will not need much help in understanding the significance of the questions which are put to the Cand. before being raised. Practically every question has been dealt with in detail in the previous books; the majority of them are taken from incidents in the Lectures and Tracing Board, and since the latter was explained at some length we shall not now detain our readers long.

The manner of preparation for the second degree stressed the masculine side, which is characteristic of it. The admission on a S. indicated that the Cand. had profited by the moral training received in the First degree, and that his conduct had always been on the S.. There is, however a deep esoteric meaning in the apparent platitude that it is the fourth part of a circle.

Among all the ancient nations the circle is a symbol of God the Infinite, Whose name we discovered in the second degree in the M.Ch., where we learnt that it consisted of four letters. Thus the Cand. was admitted on one letter of the Mystic Name, and if the four Sq.s are united with the circle in a peculiar way they form the cosmic cross, emblem of matter, within the circle of the Infinite.

We have in the last book considered at such length what is implied by the words "Hidden mysteries of nature and science," that we need here only refer our readers to that section, wherein we saw that in former times these hidden mysteries undoubtedly referred to certain occult powers, which would be dangerous if acquired by a man who had not proved himself to be of the highest moral character.

The "wages" we receive consist of the power to comprehend the nature of God, Who resides in the M.Ch. of the Soul of every Mason. The F.C. receives his wages without scruple or diffidence because the Spiritual benefit he receives from Freemasonry is in exact proportion to his desire, and ability, to comprehend its inner meaning.

He cannot receive either more or less than he has earned, for if he has not understood the profound lesson of the Divinity within him, naturally he cannot benefit therefrom.

His employers are the Divine Trinity, of Whom Justice is one of the outstanding attributes. God could not be unjust and remain God. This conception is almost a platitude, but the average man, while realising that God will not withhold any reward earned, is at times apt to assume that because God is love He will reward us more than we deserve.

This is clearly a mistake, for God could not be partial without ceasing to be God, therefore the F.C. receives exactly the Spiritual wages he has earned, and neither more nor less, but some F.C.'s will nevertheless obtain a greater reward than others, because spiritually they have earned it.

The significance of the names of the P....rs was explained in the last book, but in view of the nature of the third degree it seems advisable to point out once more that their secret Kabalistic meaning is (1) Being fortified by every moral virtue, (2) you are now properly prepared, (3) to undergo that last and greatest trial which fits you to become a M M.. Thus we see that even the w..ds of the preceding degrees lead up to this, the last and greatest.

As in the former case, the remark of the W.M. that he will put other questions if desired indicates the possibility of members of the Lodge asking questions based on the Lectures of the Second Degree, or even on the Tracing Board. It is, indeed, a pity that this right is practically never exercised. For example, a particularly appropriate question would be "What was the name of the man who cast the two great p....rs ? " As it is, the Cand. in a dramatic way represents the closing incidents in the life of this great man, whose importance till then he has hardly had any opportunity of realising.

Having answered these test questions, the cand. is again entrusted with a P.W., etc., to enable him to enter the Lodge after it has been raised to the Third degree during this temporary absence. We have in the previous book explained that the raising of a Lodge should alter the vibrations of those present by a process well recognised in the ceremonies of Magic, and, to enable the Cand. quickly to become in ttme with these higher spiritual vibrations, a word of "power" is given him, which in a moment places him on the same plane as the other members of the Lodge.

This word he has to give, not only outside the d....r of the Lodge, but also immediately before his presentation by the S.W. as "Properly prepared to be raised to the Third Degree." It is only after this has been done that the real ceremony of the Third Degree, so far as the c. is concerned, begins, and therefore that the full force of the vibrations of the M.M.'s come into play.

The P.W. itself is of the greatest significance, more especially when combined with the P.W. leading from the First to the Second degree. At one time the P.W.'s were reversed. T.C. being the W. leading to the Second, and Sh... . the W. leading to the Third. This is still the case in those foreign Grand Lodges, such as the Dutch and the French, which derive from us before 1740, when the W.s were altered owing to certain un-authorised revelations.

This alteration was one of the just grievances which brought about the secession of the so-called "Ancients," who charged Grand Lodge with altering the Ancient Landmarks. When the Irish followed our example they continued the prohibition of the introduction of m..ls until the Third degree, which is a logical procedure, for clearly you have no right to bring them into Lodge until you have been symbolically introduced to the first artificer in that material.

As the W.s now stand they convey the following spiritual lesson:- the F.C. is one who finds the simple necessities of life, such as C. and W., sufficient for his requirements. They are plenty to the spiritually minded man, whose soul becomes clogged and hampered by the acquistion of worldly possessions and since it is hard for a rich man to enter the Kingdom of Heaven, immediatdy the Cand. has symbolically received W.P. he is Sl....n.

T.C. conveys the lesson that W.P. in themselves bring death to the soul and prevent its upward progress. To-day, the river of death connected with the P.W. leading to the Second degree has largely lost its significance, whereas when it was a P.W. leading to the Third, it was in itself a fine allegory.

We must remember that Bunyan's Pilgrim's Progress was well known and widely read at the beginning of the 18th Century, and those who were re-organising our rituals at that time could not have been blind to the similarity of the allegory hidden in the w. Sh. and the account by Bunyan of Christian's fording the river of death on the way to the Holy City.

The change of about 1740 destroyed this allegory, and its survival in the Tracing Board is now merely one of those numerous footnotes which, to the careful student, are invaluable indications of the various transformations though which our ritual has passed during the course of years. Nevertheless, I do not regret the change, as I think the present spiritual lesson is even finer than the former one, but the other arrangement was more logical.

Firstly, from the practical point of view the F.C. required the use of m..l tools to perform his operative tasks, and in the process of his work acquired W.P., in contradiction to the E.A., who did only rough work and received only maintenance: i.e., corn, wine , and oil. Secondly, from the symbolical standpoint the sequence was also more logical, for the F.C., having acquired wealth by means of his skill, was brought to the river of d., and passed through it in the Third Degree.

According to Bro. Sanderson, in his "Examination of the Masonic Ritual," the actual translation of the Hebrew w. Sh. is an " e. of c., or a f. of w."- hence the manner in which it is depicted in a F.C.'s Lodge-while the w. T.C. in Hebrew means only a blacksmith, though another w. similarly pronounced means acquisition. Hence, as he points out, " an allegorical title has, in translating the Old Testament, been mistaken for the name of an actual person, for the name itself means `A worker in M...t...ls'"

Therefore the connection with H.A.B. is obvious. Bro. Sanderson, quoting from the "Secret Discipline," by S. L. Knapp, says, "In a work on ancient ecclesiastical history the following occurs, 'By a singular plasus linguae the moderns have substituted T.C. in the Third Degree for tymboxein-to be entombed.' " While I am unable to say whether Knapp is justified in this statement, it is quitee probable that this P.W., and indeed all the P.W.s are comparatively modern substitutes, taken from the Bible to replace ancient W.s of power whose full meaning was lost and whose form in consequence had become corrupt and unintelligible.

The Greek word tymboxein would be peculiariy suitable for a P.W. leading to the Third Degree, in view of its meaning, and mediaeval magical ceremonies are full of corrupt Greek words indiscriminately mingled with equally corrupt Hebrew and Arabic. There is, therefore, nothing intrinsically improbable in the suggestion that this ancient Greek word was the original from which T.C. has been evolved.

We know as a fact that large pieces of Biblical history were imported wholesale into our rituals in the 18th Century, and what is more likely than that an unintelligible work, already so corrupt as not even to be recognisable as Greek, should be amended into a well known Biblical character? However, the word as it stands, because of its Hebrew meaning of acquisition, can correctly be translated as W.P., while as meaning an artificer in M. it clearly refers to H.A.B., who made the two p.....rs, and whom the Cand. is to represent.

Thus, following this line of interpretation, we perceive that the Cand. really represents H.A.B. when he enters the Lodge, although under the disguised title conveyed by the P.W..

In dealing with these P.W.s I have endeavoured to show that there are meanings within meanings, and the same is true of practically every important incident in the whole ceremony. In a book of thissize it is obviously impossible to attempt to give all of these meanings, and even if one did the result would be to befog the young reader and so prevent him from getting a clear and connected interpretation of the ceremony.

It is for this reason that, in the main, I am concentrating on one line of interpretation, but I have thought it desirable in this section to give a hint to more advanced students, so that they can follow up similar lines of investigation for themselves.

PREPARATION

In English and Scotch workings there is no c.t. around the Cand. in preparation for the Third Degree, but in the Irish working it is wound once around his n., in the Second degree twice, and the First three times. If we regard the c.t. as symbolising those things which hamper a man's spiritual progress, the gradual unwinding of it as used in Irish workings becomes of great significance.

This interpretation implies that the Cand. is hampered in Body, Soul and Spirit in the First Degree, whereas by the time he has reached this point in the Third Degree the Body and Soul have triumphed over the sins which peculiarly assail them, and in that stage symbolised by the Degree itself the Spirit has only to triumph over Spiritual sins, such as Spiritual Pride. With this exception the manner of preparation is the same in all these British workings, and indicates that the Cand. is now about to consecrate both sides of his nature, active and passive, creative and preservative, etc., to the service of the Most High.

The explanation already given in the previous books of the various details, such as being s.s., holds here, and a brief glance at the other volumes will render it unnecessary for me to take up valuable space therewith in this third book. The Can. is then brought to the Lodge door and gives the Kn.s of a F.C. These Kn's indicate that Soul and Body are in union, but the Spirit is still out of contact whereas the proper Kn's of a M.M. (2/1) indicates that the Spirit dominates the Soul and is in union with it, the body having fallen away into significance.

It will be remembered that in the first book of this series I pointed out that the three separate kn's of an E.A. symbolise that in the uninitiated man, Body, Soul and Spirit are all at variance. Meanwhile the Lodge has been raised to a Third Degree by a ceremony whose profound significance demands consideration in a separate chapter.

CHAPTER II.

THE OPENING

Having satisfied himself that all present are symbolically upright and moral men, the W.M. asks the J.W. if his spiritual nature has evolved sufficiently to control both soul and body. The J.W. suggests that he should be tested, not only by the emblem of upright conduct, but also by the Compasses. Now these combined with the Square form a lozenge, which is itself a symbol for the Vesica Piscis, emblem of the female principle.

The Compasses, moreover, are the instruments with which geometrical figures are created, and more especially the Circle. By means of two circles the triangle, emblem of the triune nature of God,. is produced, while the Cirde itself is the emblem of Eternity and therefore of Spirit. A point within the cirle forms the symbol for the Hindu conception of the Supreme Being, Paramatma, whence we have come and whither we shall all ultimately return.

At the centre of the circle rests all knowledge; there shall we find every lost secret. Now such a figure can only be drawn with the help of the Compasses, and in drawing it the following significant symbolical act takes place.

One point of the Compass rests at the centre, and the other makes the circle of the Infinite. No matter how far the legs of the Compass be extended, or how large the Circle, the fact remains that one leg is always at the centre. Thus the Compasses, while they travel through infinity, are at the same time never separated from the centre, and from that point cannot err.

This instrument may therefore be considered as standing for the Divine Spark in Man, in all its manifestations. One of these is conscience; but the Divine Spark has many attributes and names.

So the J.W.'s reply indicates that he is prepared to be tested both by the moral code and by the spiritual laws of our being.

But after these preliminaries the proceedings become of an even more exalted nature. All that has gone before has been but preparation for the Great Quest on which we must now set forth. It is the quest of the Soul for realisation of God, and at-one-ment with Him. This is the Mystic Quest of all ages, and, true to the ancient symbolism, it starts from the East, the place of Light, and goes towards the West, the place of darkness and death.

The East represents God, Who is our home. It indicates that each soul comes out from the place of Light, from Light itself, that is, from the very substance of God, descends through the Gateway of the Dawn and becomes incarnate in Matter. But it brings with it a sense of loss and separation, for it has come out from God, and the Divine Spark within it longs return whence it came.

Having lost the secret of its true nature and the way of return, it wanders in darkness, seeking and for most men the way of return is through the

Western portal, the gateway of Death, for so long as we are finite beings we cannot hope to comprehend the Infinite.

Yet there are some few exceptions to the general rule, who, while still in the flesh, have a vision of the Divine splendour, are caught up in it, and became one with God. To such men the return to ordinary mundane existence seems unreal and shadowy. Where others believe in God they Know Him, but it is almost impossible for them to convey to others the experience through which they have gone. Yet that such experiences are real, as real as any other fact in life, is attested by a long line of witnesses right throughout the ages.

To the average man, however, the first real step towards the realisation of what constitutes God is through the portal of physical death; - but even then the end is still far off.

Hence the answer explaining how the true secrets came to be lost indicates, not the cause of the loss, but the first step towards the recovery, and this fact is borne out by the subsequent events in the ceremony itself.

Note, it is the body only that dies, and by its death enables the Soul and Spirit to re-discover in part the secrets which were last. Yet this death of the Body effectually debars the communication of these secrets to the sorrowing F.C.'s left behind. It is the passing through that veil which separates life and death which stars us on the road which ends with God.

It must never be forgotten, however, that the genuine secrets are never recovered in the Craft, although symbolically we rise from the grave, for that secret can only be discovered at or with the C.-i.e., with God. To that exalted position we can only attain after long journeys through the planes of existence beyond the grave. In our symbolism there is nothing which indicates that immediately after death man is fit to pass into the presence of the King of Kings.

But the Divine Spark within us is never really separated from the Great and All-Pervading Spirit. It is still part of it, though its glory is dimmed by the veil of flesh. Therefore, just as one arm of the compasses ever rests on the centre, no matter how far the other leg travels; so however far we may travel from God, and however long and hard may be the journey, the Divine Spark within us can never be truly separated from Him, or err from that Centre. Thus the point of the Compasses at the centre of the circle may be considered to be the Spirit, the head of the Compasses the Soul, and the point on the circumference the body.

So the task is set and the brethren go forth on the quest, that quest which must lead through the darkness of death, as the ceremony that follows tells in allegory. It is not correct to say that the search hinted at in the Opening ceremony is suddenly abandoned, and those who think this misinterpret the whole meaning of the legend.

Never in earthly life shall we find the answer we seek, nay, even death itself will not give it; but, having passed beyond the grave, through the four veils of the Scottish rite, and so into the H.R.A., we find an excellent answer in allegorical and symbolical language, whilst the jewel of the degree emphasises what the end of the quest is.

Nor must it be forgotten that the body alone cannot realise the nature of God, and that is why without the help of the other two, H.A.B. neither could, nor would, disclose the S........t.

The W.M.'s promise to help indicates that the Spirit will render assistance, but though the Spirit subsequently raises man from the grave it is not sufficiently evolved to give him the true secret. This can only come about when the Spirit has raised the Soul to a far higher stage of spirituality.

Though this is the degree of Destruction, that form of the Trinity is not invoked, and the title used corresponds more closely to the Hindu name for the All-Embracing than to their form of the Destroyer. This no doubt is deliberate, for the symbol of this degree is the same emblem which among the Hindus denotes the Most High, namely the Circle with a Point within it.

In some Scotch rituals, after the Lodge has been opened in the first degree the I.P.M., or the D.C., opens the V.S.L., and, strange to say, does so with the words, "In the beginning was the Word." Similarly, when the Lodge is closed in the first degree the book is closed with the words, "And the word was with God."

Here then we get two striking features: I) the use of words from the first chapter of the Gospel according to St. John, and 2) their correlation with the phrase in the Third Degree, "At, or with the C." This procedure suggests that the lost W. is the Logos, or Christ, and remembering what we have previously pointed out in the earlier books, i.e., that there is a perfectly logical Christian interpretation of the whole of the Craft ceremonies, this fact becomes of increasing significance.

Before closing this chapter, I would like to add that the Third Degree lends itself to a Christian interpretation even more markedly than the former ones, and several of the higher degrees in Freemasonry adopt and expand this line of teaching.

In view of the fact that in the Middle Ages Freemasonry was undoubtedly Christian, we cannot lightly reject this view of the inner meaning of the ceremonies, but as the frame work of our ceremonies apparently goes back before Christian times, a non-Christian interpretation is equally permissible.

CHAPTER III.

THE SYMBOLICAL JOURNEYS, ETC.

The Can. is admitted on he C....... s, and this fact is of far greater significance than most brethren probably realise. Firstly, as has been noted, one arm of the C.s is always at the C., no matter how far the other may travel, and from the point of view of the Can., though he knows it not, this act in a sense indicates that his heart, and therefore he himself, is at or on the C........e. Secondly, the C....s in this degree link up with the Sq. used in the former degree on a similar occasion.

We have seen in the previous books that the Sq. and C........s are united on the Ped. in such a way as to form the vesica piscis, the emblem of the female principle, and the symbol of birth and rebirth. Hence symbolically the Can. passes through the vesica piscis. Also after entering the Lodge in this, as in the previous degrees, he kn....s while the blessing of Heaven is invoked, and as he does so the wands of the deacons are crossed above his head.

He thus kn........s in a triangle, the emblem of Spirit, and itself connected with the lozenge. Two equilateral triangles make a lozenge, which is produced from the vesica piscis-formed by two circles, as shown by the first proposition in Euclid. In view of the great stress laid upon Geometry throughout the whole of our rituals these facts cannot be ignored. Our Operative Brn. must have realised that the whole science of Geometry arises out of this first proposition, which shows how to make a triangle (the emblem of the Trinity and the Spirit) by means of two circles whose circumferences pass through the centre of each other.

In doing so they form the vesica piscis, which gives birth first of all to the triangle, and secondly, to the double triangle, in the form of a lozenge. This last emblem is symbolised by the sq., denoting matter, and the c...s, denoting spirit. The above facts throw a flood of light upon the interplay between these Masonic emblems.

Before leaving this subject it is worth while pointing out that the Can. likewise takes every Ob. in Craft masonry within this triangle, and that the same method is employed in other ancient rites, including those of the Society of Heaven and Earth in China, where the Can. kn...s on one sword, while two others are held over his head so as to form a triangle of steel.

The Can. now starts on his three symbolical journeys. He first satisfies the J.W., representing the Body, that he is an E.A., i.e., a man of good moral character. He next satisfies the S.W., representing the Soul, that he has benefited by the lessons of life and acquired intellectual knowledge. Then comes the third journey, when he is once more challenged by the Soul, who demands the P.W., the full significance of which has already been explained. Let us combine these meanings! He comes laden with worldly possessions, which in themselves carry the seeds of death, unconsciously representing in his person the worker in metals who made the twin colunms, and is about to be entombed. (tymboxein).

Therefore the Soul presents him to the Spirit as one properly prepared to carry out the part of his great predecessor. There is a point here which we need to realise, for it is one which is often overlooked. In the previous degrees only one Deacon was instructed to lead the Can. by the proper S...ps to the E., but here both are needed.

From the practical point of view there is no obvious reason why the help of the J.D. should be invoked at all, and as the ceremony is usually carried out he does nothing but look on. I believe, however, the S.D. should first go through the S...ps and the J.D., should assist the Can. to copy his example. If thus were so we should get an almost exact repetition of the analogous ceremony in the R.A. where the p.s., corresponding to the S.D., is helped by an assistant.

Thus, with the Can., in both cases we get a Trinity, only one of whom actually descends into the g., or, in the other case, into the v. As Major Sanderson has pointed out in An Examination of the Masonic Ritual, among the primitive, races usually, a man who stepped over an o.g. would be considered to have committed sacrilege, and almost certainly would be slain, but, on the other hand, we do know that in many Initiatory Rites either the Can., or someone else for him, steps down into a gr., and is subsequently symbolically sl...n therein.

If this be the true interpretation of this part of the ceremony, the reason for the presence of the two deacons in addition to the Can. becomes clear. It is only the Body that descends into the clear the Soul and the Spirit have no part therein. Thus, for the moment, though only temporarily, these three represene the triune nature of man, while the three principal officers represent the triune nature of God. The fact that this is undoubtedly true in the case of the R.A., makes it almost certain that the same idea underlies this apparently unimportant diffirence between the arrangements in the third degree, and those followed in the first and second.

Again and again when one comes to study carefully the details of our ritual, one finds little points, such as these, which would certainly not have survived the drastic revision of 1816 if there had not been present some men who really did understand the inner meaning of our ceremonies, and refused to allow important lessons to be lost by the removal of what, at first sight, appear to be unnecessary details.

Therefore, those of us who value the inner meaning of our ceremonies owe a deep debt of gratitude to these men, even though their actual names be unknown to us, and on our part a duty is imposed on us that we shall not hastily tamper with the rituals, merely because we do not ourselves see the full significance of a phrase or think that by revising it we can make the wording run more smoothly.

The next factor we must consider most carefully is the actual sp...s themselves. These make the Latin cross of suffering and sacrifice.

Sometimes the sp..s are not done quite correctly, for the Can. should be careful to face due North, due South, and due East respectively. This procedure undoubtedly refers to the three entrances of the Temple through which H.A.B. endeavoured to escape. Hence it is we see that the Master himself trod out the cross of Calvary during the tragedy, and in a sense made the Consecration Cross of the Temple.

In a mediaeval church, and even to-day at the consecration of a church according to the Anglican ordinance, there should be a dedication cross marked on the building. In the Middle Ages these were usually marked on the pillars, and apparently corresponded to the mark made by an illiterate person when witnessing a deed.

The Consecrating Bishop sometimes drew this cross on the pillar or wall, or sometimes merely traced over a cross already painted there for the purpose. Any new piece of work in a church, even if only a new fresco, had its dedication cross. For example :-At Chaldon Church, Surrey, the dedication cross is marked on the margin of a fresco depicting The Brig of Dread, described at length in Freemasonry and the Ancient Gods.

Bearing these facts in mind, we shall perceive that, even from the Operative point of view, the manner of advancing in this degree, and the manner in which H.A.B. met his end, had a peculiar significance. The Great Architect of the Temple must have traced the dedication cross the whole length and breadth of the Temple in his own blood. Moreover, such dedication crosses as have actually survived are nearly always found to be painted in red.

Thus, H.A.B.'s last work was, as it were, to commence the consecration of the Temple which was completed by K.S., for until that cross had been marked either on the wall or pavement, according to mediaeval Operative ideas the building could not be consecrated. Therefore, the Can., who is reenacting the same drama, must obviously do likewise, and in so doing dedicates the Temple of his body.

But there is still more hidden within this ceremonial act. The ancient Knights Templar were accused of trampling on the cr., and a careful examination of the evidence taken at the trial shows that in reality they took a ritual sp., somewhat similar to those taken by the Can. in this degree.

One of the esoteric meanings indicated is the Way of the Cross which leads to Calvary. Furhermore, having thus traced out a cr. he is subsequendy laid on it, and this fact is emphasised by the position in which his legs or feet are placed. The foot of this cr. reaches to the Ped., on which rests the O.T.

If, therefore, this symbolical cr. were raised as it was on Calvary it would rest on the O.T., and the Can. would face the E., and would be, as it were, on a mountain. This fact should be borne in mind by those who seek a Christian interpretation of our Craft ceremonies. Mystically interpreted, it indicates that every aspirant for union with the Divine must tread the Way of the Cross, and suffer and die thereon, in order that he may rise to a new life, a realisation of his union with the Infinite.

Even those who are disinclined to admit the possibility of a Christian interpretatior, of the Craft degrees, must recognise the fact that this cr. is the cr. of sacrifice and means that the true aspirant must be prepared to sacrifice everything in his search after Truth.

The number of the sp...s is the combination of the Trinity and of the four elements, representing matter. It is the same number as forms the perfect lodge, and also the seven elements which form man, whether we interpret it according to the ancient Egyptian system, or in the more modern form of the five physical senses, the Soul and the Spirit. In the latter case it indicates that the man must be prepared to sacrifice, or shall we say dedicate to God, Body, Soul and Spirit.

There are yet other profound meanings in this one ritual act, but enough has been written to set my readers pondering for themselves, and we will therefore proceed to consider the next point in the ceremony.

The Ob. itself contains one or two interesting points. Thus it indicates that a M.M.'s Lodge must always be open on the C.. This shows us at once that we are dealing with a ceremony with a mystical meaning, for the C. means the same as the middle ch. in the second degree-the secret chamber of the heart, where dwells the Divine Spark-and so tells us in veiled language that all that happens thereafter is a spiritual experience, which sooner or later comes to every mystic.

The special moral obligations which the Can. undertakes should be noted, but require no explanation. It is, however, difficult to understand why they should be deferred until this stage. In the ancient charges similar obligations are imposed apparently on the E.A., and this seems more logical.

The Py. varies even in different parts of England, but in essentials is always the same. You are s. at the c., and the manner of disposal is very reminiscent of the way in which the dead are cremated in India in honour of Shiva. There the corpse is burnt near running water, preferably near the Ganges, and the ashes are thrown into the air over the river to the four cardinal points, that the winds may scatter them. It must be remembered that Shiva represents the destructive attribute of the Diety and he makes the P.S. of a M.M. on his statues. His is the element of fire, and all these facts must be born in mind when considering our own Py.

The position of the Sq. and Cs., in addition to the explanation given, indicates that the spirit, represented by the Cs., now dominates the body, typified by the Sq..

CHAPTER IV.

THE EXHORTATION

The opening part of the exhortation gives a convenient summary of the previous degress and quite clearly indicates that the first inner meaning of the series is Birth, Life which is of course educational and preparatory for its sequel, and Death. The phrase relating to the second degree "And to trace it, from its devlopment through the paths of Heavenly Science even to the throne of God Himself," shows plainly its real significance. As pointed out in the F.C. Handbook, in the Mid. Ch. the F.C. discovers not only the name of God, but that he himself is the fifth letter Shin which transforms the name Jehovah into the name Jeheshue, or Messias, the King.

But according to the old Kabala Jeheshue must be raised on the cross of Tipareth, and the significance of this fact is impressed on our Can. by the incidents now to take place. The average Christian need not trouble about the subtleties of the Kabala, for the story in the New Testament supplies him with a very similar interpretation.

The W.M. having, almost casually, given him this key to the inner meaning of what is about to follow, proceeds at once to the most dramatic part of the ceremony. Up to this point almost all forms of our ritual are practically the same, but henceforward there are many marked differences.

"Emulation" ritual may be regarded as containing the bare minimum, but the additional details found in many Provincial workings in England, and in Scotland, Ireland, America, and many of the Continental Lodges, are too important to be ignored. There is no reason to assume that they are innovations; on the contrary all the evidence points to the fact that they are integral parts of the ceremony which, for various reasons, were omitted by the revisers of our ritual who met in the Lodge of Reconciliation. I shall therefore proceed to note and explain them where necessary.

Whereas in Emulation working as soon as the Ws. are called on the deacons retire, in most others, in the Provinces, etc., they fall back to the head of the g.. Thus with the W.M. the W.s form the triangle of Spirit, and with the D.s the Sq. of matter, on which the triangle rests, for the M. descends from his chair and stands in front of the Ped..

As a practical piece of advice I would recommend that the J.W. should not direct the Can. to c. his f. until after the S.W. has dealt with him, for it is impossible for him to drop on his respective k...s if his f. are c., whereas by carrying out these instructions before the last attack he will fall the more readily.

In most of the old Scotch rituals the Can. journeys round the Lodge, is attacked by the J.W. in the S., by the S.W. in the W. (note that), and returns to the M. in the E., where the final incident takes place. I think, however, our English system of having the attack in the N. instead of in the W. is preferable, and is probably the correct form. In the Scotch ritual the three villains have names, and the same is the case in America.

They are Jubela, Jubelo, and Jubelum. The word itself clearly comes from the Latin word meaning "To command," and refers to the fact that they commanded him to give up the S....s. But the terminations of the three names appear to have a curious esoteric reference to India. It can hardly be by accident that these three names form the mystic word AUM.

The U in India in this case is pronounced almost like O, and when this word is disguised, as it usually is, it is written OMN. If this be so we have the Creative Preservative, and Annihilative aspects of the Deity emphasised in the Third Degree, and it is the Destructive aspect, symbolised by the letter M, which deals the final stroke.

This variation is therefore of importance, but I must warn my readers that not all Scotch workings have it, some of them being much more akin to our own, even having the attack in the N.. Practically all of them, however, have the perambulations, during which solemn music is played. The usual procedure is for the brethren to pass round the gr. once making the P. S. of an E.A.. When this is done the J.W. makes his abortive attempt.

The second round is made with the H. S. of an F.C., after which the S.W. tries and fails. The third round is made with the S. of G. and D. of a M.M., on the conclusion of which the Can. is r... by the lion's g.... It is a great pity that the use of this name for the M. M.'s g. is falling into disuse in London, for it has in itself important symbolical references, to which we shall refer later in the chapter.

In many parts of England it is still customary to place the Can., either in a c----n or in a g. made in the floor, and the same method is found in most other parts of the world. Indeed, in the Dutch ritual the Can. is first of all shown a c..n in which is a human skeleton. This is subsequently removed, though he does not know it and he thinks when he is laid therein he will find himself in its bony clutches. Even as near London as Windsor there is a Masonic Temple which has a special chamber of d. with a g. actually in the floor and until recently it was still used although whether it is to-day I cannot say.

Let us now turn to consider the meanings of the main incidents. The first meaning of the degree is obvious; it prepares a man for his final end and hints of a possibility of life beyond the grave but it must be admitted that the lesson is not driven home with the same force as it is in most of the ancient mysteries.

Osiris Himself rose from the dead and became the Judge of all who followed after Him, and because of this fact His worshippers believed that they too would rise. In our legend, however, it is only the dead body of H.A.B. which is lifted out of the g. in a peculiar manner, and in the legend there is not even a hint as to what befell his Soul. The question is often asked why they should have raised a c..s and placed it on its feet. (1)

90

(I) See Ward, Who Was Hiram Abiff?

One explanation probably is, by analogy with the Greek story of the manner in which Hercules recovered Alcestis and ransomed her from the bondage of Thanatos-Death himself. We are told that Hercules wrestled with Thanatos and would nor let him go until he had agreed to allow Hercules to bring her back from the realm of the Shades to the land of living men.

It may be that the corpse here represents Death. It is also worth noting that Isis joined together the fragments of the body of Osiris, and the "Setting up" of the backbone of the God was a ceremony carried out every year by the ancient Egyptian Priests. The body of Osiris apparently was raised from the bier by Anubis in precisely the same way as the M.M. is r.. When it was set on its feet life returned to it.

One fact is certain, that in every Rite which has as its central theme symbolic d. the Can. is r. by the same g., and in precisely the same manner, and this manner becomes a method of greeting and of recognition among all who have passed through this type of ceremony. For example :-it is known and used in the Dervish Rite, among West African Negroes, among the Red Indians of Central America, and was apparently known to the ancient Druids, for it is carved on a stone found at Iona. In the ancient rites of Mithra it also appears to have been the method used upon a similar occasion. These facts show that it is an ancient landmark and one to be most carefully guarded.

The use of the phrase The Lion Grip is peculiarly significant, as Major Sanderson shows in his work, An Examination of the Masonic Ritual. Therein he points out that in the Book of the Dead the Supreme God, whether Ra or Osiris, is appealed to as the " God in the Lion form," and in all such cases the prayer of the Soul is that he may be permitted to " Come forth " in the East, rising with the sun from the d..s of the g..

In Egypt the lion was the `personification of strength and power, but it is usually associated with the idea of the regeneration of the Sun, and therefore with the resurrection. Major Anderson goes on to point out as follows. "Shu (Anheru, `the Lifter') who as the light of the Dawn was said to lift up the sky-goddess from the arms of the sleeping Earth, is often represented as a lion, for only through him was the rebirth of the Sun made possible.

Osiris is called the lion of yesterday, and Ra the Lion of tomorrow : the bier of Osiris is always represented as having the head and legs of a lion." Thus as Major Sanderson indicates, the expression "the lion grip" is a survival from, the Solar cult, and therefore a landmark which should be carefully preserved.

The Bright Morning Star whose rising brings peace and Salvation, almost certainly was originally Sirius, but to Englishmen it must seem strange that Sirius should be said to bring peace and Salvation. The association of these ideas with the Dog Star is undoubtedly a fragment which has come down from Ancient Egypt, for the rising of Sirius marked the beginning of the inundation of the Nite, which literally brought salvation to the people of Egypt by irrigating the land and enabling it to produce food.

That Sirius was an object of veneration to the philosophers of the ancient world is well known to all archaeologists, and many of the Temples in Egypt have been proved to have been oriented on Sirius. There is also a good deal of evidence showing that some of the stone circles in Great Britain were similarly oriented on Sirius by the Druids.

It is therefore not surprising that this star is still remembered in our rituals. Naturally it has acquired a deeper spiritual meaning in the course of years, and may be regarded as representing the First Fruits of the Resurrection, the sure hope of our Redemption. This aspect is set forth in the lectures drawn up by Dunckerley, who regarded it as the star of Bethlehem, and as typifying Christ. See Rev. xxii, 16.

At this point the Can.. who has been carefully put in the N., the place of darkness, is moved round by the right to the South. From the practical point of view this is to enable the M. to re-enter his chair from the proper side, but there is also an inner meaning. Immediately after death the Soul is said to find itself on the earth plane amid murk and darkness.

Lacking mortal eyes, it cannot perceive the sun, and, on the other hand, is still so immersed in matter that it cannot yet see clearly with its spirit eyes; but this stage rapidly passes away, and the Soul is received into a higher plane of existence, being brought thither by messengers of Light. The position in the North represents this period of darkness on the earth plane, and that this is not accidental is shown by the fact that in most rituals the lights are not turned up until the phrase "That bright morning star, etc." has been uttered.

Then the M., representing one of these spirit messengers, leads the Can. gently round to the South, thereby symboling his entry into the place of light. And who is this messenger? Every installed master who has received the P.W. leading to the Chair should realise that, no matter how unworthy, he represents the risen Christ. Thus we see the peculiarly appropriate nature of the act coming after the reference to the bright morning star, which also in another sense represents the risen Christ.

CHAPTER V.

THE S....TS

Having thus been brought into the place of light the Can. is given not the Gen. Ss, but only substitued ones. This fact must often have puzzled the Can.. The pratical reason given in the ritual, though perfecdy inteligible to a R.A. mason, cannot be the real one. In view of the unexpected calamity no-one could have thought K.S. was breaking his ob. by nominating a successor to H.A.B. and giving him the full ss..ts.

Actually according to the R.A. story he did something much worse, for he wrote them down and placed them somewhere, in the hopes that they would be subsequently rediscovered, and he had no assurance that their discoverers would even be masons, much less that they would keep their discovery secret. Of course this is also an allegory, and from this stand-point perfectly correct. The lost s...ts are the nature and attributes of God, which must be realised by each man for himself, and no other man can really communicate them.

Moreover, this complete realisation of the nature of God, and the union of the Divine Spark within us with the Source of All, can never be achieved during mortal life. Even after death we shall need to leave the world long behind and travel far, before we can hope to attain that state of spiritual evolution which will enable us to approach the Holy of Holies, and gaze with unveiled eyes upon Him, Who is the beginning and the end of all.

With regard to these substituted s..ts. let us note that they grow out of those used by the F.C.. Having already shown in the last book that the sn.s of the F.C., and in fact the real s..t of that degree, is the transformation of Jehovah into Jeheshue,

we see that this is most appropriate. To use modern language, the second degree teaches of the birth of the Christ Spirit within us, while the third indicates that mystically we, like the great Master, must die and rise again. As St. Paul says, " Die daily in Christ."

The sn.s given are probably all of great antiquity. Of some we have evidence which shows that they were venerated in ancient Egypt and Mexico, are still employed in the primitive Initiatory Rites of the savages, and are associated with the Gods in India. For example, the P.S. is used by Shiva, the Great Destroyer, Who when He makes it, holds in His hand the lariet of death.

The sn. of G. and D. is found all round the world, as I have shown in full detail in Sign Language of the Ancient Mysteries. Ancient Mexico, where Quetzacoatl makes it, can be matched with Easter Island in the far Pacific, Peru, West Africa, East Africa, New Guinea, Malaya and many other places.

Major Sanderson points out that the second Cas. Sn. is depicted in Egyptian pictures as being used by those who are saluting Osiris in his coffin. Those who desire will find it in Papyrus 9,908 in the British Museum.

The English sn. of g. and d. (for up till now we have been speaking of the Scotch form) is almost certainly not the correct one. Its general appearance would incline one to believe that it is a penal sn., though whence derived it is difficult to say. A little thought will indicate the nature of the penalty as being somewhat similar to that of one of the higher degrees.

So far as I can find it is not recognised as a sn. of g. and d. to-day, except among masons who are descended masonically from the Grand Lodge of England, but in a picture by Guercino of Christ cleansing the Temple, in the Palazzo Rosso, Crenoa, both this and the Scotch form are shown, while the G. of H. constantly appears in mediaeval paintings, e.g., in the Raising of Lazarus. (I)

(I) see The Sign Language of the Mysteries by Ward.

The so-called Continental form undoubtedly comes from a well known high degree, where it is much more appropriate: it is apparently restricted to the Latin countries, whereas even in Germany it is the Scotch form that is employed.

The sn. of Exul. is a form used to this day in of Asia to indicate worship, and was similarly employed in Ancient Egypt. Major Sanderson suggests that it was copied from the position in which Shu upheld the sky.

Thus we see that six out of the so-called seven sn.s can be shown to be of ancient origin, and it is quite probable that further research will enable us to prove that the other one is equally old. Such sn.s as these originally had a magical significance, and the explanation given in the ritual as to their

origin is no doubt of a much later date than the sn.s themselves. Indeed, a careful study of certain of the sn.s will show that they are not the natural sn.s which would have been used to indicate the feeling they are said to express. For example, in the sn. of h...r the left hand would not naturally be placed in the position in which we are taught to put it, if this sn. had originated as related in. the story.

So obvious is this that some modern preceptors of Lodges of Instruction have to my knowledge altered the position of the left hand in order to make it conform to the story, but I venture to think that in so doing they are committing a very serious mistake, nothing less than the removal of an ancient landnrark.

Some day we shall probably discover the real origin of this sn., but if it is altered that will of course become impossible.

The lion's grip and the actual position of r..s...g are equally old, and, so far as we can find, this manner of r..s...g is employed in every rite, whether ancient or primitive, which deals with the dramatic representation of d.. As a manner of greeting it is employed by the initiated men in many Red Indian Trihes, in West Africa, among the Senussi in North Africa, and in the Dervish Rites. (I)

(I) For further explanation see Ward, Who Was Hiram Abiff?

The parts of the b. brought in contact with each other are all parts presided over by some sign of the Zodiac, and there would appear to be some old astrological meaning which has now become lost. It may possibly have been connected with Gemini, the Twins, and this fact is made the more probable by the survival of the name "The Ln's Gr."

The explanation given, although possibly of a fairly recent origin, nevertheless contains a valuable inner meaning, for it shows that we cannot hope to advance towards God unless we do our duty to our fellow men. Thus in dramatic form is shown that the brotherhood of man necessitates the Fatherhood of God.

It hardly seems necessary in this book to point out again that the regular st. forms a tau cross and teaches us that we must trample under foot our animal passions, if we desire to approach near to God. We note, however, that the Can., in advancing to obtain the s..ts, has perforce to make three tau crosses, and the Christian Mystic will

(1) For further explanation see Ward, Who Was Hiram Abiff?

doubtless perceive in this a hidden reference to the three crosses on Calvary.

Finally, as has already been pointed out, the penalties of the first and second degrees draw attention to two important occult centres, and so also in this degree the Solar Plexus, the most important occult centre of all, is indicated, and since the object of every Mystic is to achieve the Beatific vision, the fact that the monks of Mt. Athos, near Salonica, do so by fixing their eye on this part, shows that there is a very special reason for the special form of the p.s of the third degree.

CHAPTER VI.

THE BADGE

On his re-entering the Lodge the Can. is presented, and in due course invested by the S.W., as in the previous degrees, thereby indicating that even after death man's spiritual advancement is registered by the Soul. The Badge itself, however, is full of symbolic meaning, and though in its present form it is of comparatively recent date, it is evident that those who designed it had a much deeper knowledge of symbolism than some modern critits are apt to believe.

Firstly, the colour, which is that of Cambridge University, and likewise that used by Parliament when fighting King Charles, has a much deeper significance than is generally known. It is closely related to the colour of the Virgin Mary, which itself had been brought forward from Isis and the other Mother Goddesses of the ancient world.

It is possible that the designers were also influenced by the existence of certain Orders of Knighthood which had their appropriate colours, for the aprons of Grand Lodge Officers have Garter blue, but this blue is also the colour of Oxford, and the colour associated with the Royalist cause at the time of the Civil War. At any rate, it is appropriate that our aprons should thus employ the colours of the two great Universities of England.

There is, of course, an exception in the case of the red aprons allocated to Grand Stewarts, for which there are historical reasons into which we need not now enter. We may, however point out that the dark blue aprons of Grand Lodge are often, though erroneously, spoken of as the Purple, indicating a Royal colour, and thereby implying no doubt that Brn. entitled to wear this colour are rulers in the Craft, and represent the masculine element.

Light blue, on the other hand, represents the feminine or passive aspect, and is most appropriate for the ordinary M.M., whose duty it is to obey, and not to command. Indeed, the M.M.'s apron contain: other emblems which indicate this feminine aspect. These are the three rosettes, which symbolise the rose, itself a substitute for the Vesica Piscis, and they are arranged so as to form a triangle with the point upwards, interpenetrating the triangle formed by the flap of the apron.

The two triangles only interpenetrate half way, therein differing from the double triangles seen on the jewels worn by R. A. Masons, which completely overlap. These two triangles deserve a little careful study. The lower triangle with its point upwards is the triangle of fire, the emblem of Shiva, and the symbol of the Divine Spark. The triangle made by the flap of the apron, which has its point directed downwards, is the triangle of water, and is thus to some extent representative of the Soul.

These two triangles are within a sq., the emblem of matter, and therefore of the body, and so we see that the M.M.'s apron symbolically represents the triune nature of man, whereas the R.A. jewel, (the only high degree jewel which may be worn in a Craft Lodge) has these two triangles within a circle, which is the emblem of the Infinite. In this case the triangle of water presents the preservative aspect, the triangle of fire, the destructive aspect, the point or eye at the centre, the creative aspect, and the circle, the everlasting nature of the Supreme Being. There is therefore a curious correspondence, and also a marked difference, between the jewel of the R.A. Mason, and the apron of the M.M..

Viewed from another standpoint the apron has another set of meanings. The triangle represents Spirit, and the Sq., matter. The flap forms a triangle entering into the sq., and so depicts the entry of Spirit into matter, and therefore, man. The E.A.'s apron should have the flap pointing upward, indicating that the Divine Wisdom has not yet truly penetrated the gross matter of our bodies.

This custom is unfortunately going out of use in modern Masonry, which is a great pity, as undoubtedly a valuable lesson is thus lost. The F.C. has the flap pointing downward for several reasons. Firstly, to indicate that wisdom has begun to enter and therefore to control matter; secondly, to represent the triangle of water and thus indicate that Soul and Body are acting in unison; thirdly, because this triangle is the emblem of Vishnu the Preserver, and so emphasises - the fact that the aspect of God taught in this degree is the preservative aspect, whereas the addition of the three rosettes in the third degree shows, not only the union of Body, Soul and Spirit, but also that the great lesson of this degree is the importance of the Destructive side of the Diety, or as we may prefer to tall it, the Transformative side.

What, however, of the two rosettes worn by the F.C.? Firstly, they stress the dual nature of man, and have a very clear reference to the two p...rs. Similarly, no doubt, they indicate that the F.C. is not yet a complete and united being ; Body and Soul are in union, but unlike the M.M., these two are not in complete accord with the Spirit. Thus we obtain a correspondence between the knocks of the F.C. and the two rosettes. Furthermore, the triangle is incomplete, showring that the F.C. is not yet a complete F.M., and this correlates with the position of the C.s when taking the ob. in the F. C. degree.

Two other features of the apron must also be considered. Firstly, the tassels, which appear originately to have been the ends of the string with which the apron was bound round the waist. There is little doubt that in the 18th century the aprons had not the present symbolic tassels, but were fastened round the body in a very similar way to that in which the E.A. and F.C. aprons are to this day. It is interesting to note in this connection that the actual aprons worn by the officers of Grand Lodge for the year, as distinct from the Past Grand Officers' aprons, have no tassels at all.

In the course of years, no doubt, the ends of the strings were ornamented by tassels, and to this day the aprons of the Royal Order of Scotland are bounmd round the body by an ornamental cord with tassels, which are tied in front in such a way that the two tassels stick out from underneath the flap.

These tassels, when the final form of our aprons was fixed, were separated from the bands which fasten the apron, and attached to the apron itself, becoming as we now see simply strips of ribbon on which are fastened seven chains. When this change took place it is clear that those who made the alteration deliberately chose the number 7, and intended thereby to convey a symbolic meaning. We have already explained the numerous symbolic meanings of the number 7; for example, it represents God and Man, Spirit and Matter, etc.

Naturally they had to have two tassels to balance, and it would have been very inartistic to have had four chains on one tassel and three on the other, and so it would be unwise to lay too much stress on the number 14, which is the sum total. We may regard it merely as a curious and interesting coincidence that the body of Osiris was stated to have been divided by Set into 14 pieces.

But in addition to these details as to the historical development of the tassels, we must not forget that in many of the 18th century aprons the two p....rs are depicted. These aprons were usually decorated by paintings on the leather, and varied considerably from Lodge to Lodge, but one of the most usual kinds of decoration included the two p..rs, and the remembrance of these may very probably have influenced those who designed our present apron.

The modern arrangement by which the apron is fastened, namely, a piece of webbing with a hook and eye attachment, gave a fine opportunity for some really profound symbolism, and I feel certain that it was not an accident which led to the universal adoption of the snake to serve this purpose.

There are two kinds of symbolism attached to the snake in all ancient religions. Firstly, the snake as the enemy of man, and therefore as the representative of the powers of evil; and secondly the snake as emblem of the Divine Wisdom. " Be ye wise as serpents" does not refer to the craftiness of the Devil, but to the Divine Wisdom itself.

In Ancient Egypt the Soul as he passed through the Underworld met with serpents of evil, and also with serpents of good. In India, legend tells us of a whole order of beings, the Serpent Folk, who are of a Spiritual nature different from man, possessed their own rulers, and were endowed with superhuman wisdom. Some of these are considered to be friendly to man, while others are hostile. The Sacred Cobra is well known to every student of Hindu religions, and is essentially good.

Actual worship is paid to the Serpent throughout the whole of India, and in many other parts of the world, and in the Kapala we get clear traces of the fact that under certain circumstances the serpent is regarded as "The Shining One" -the Holy Wisdom Itself. Thus we see that the serpent on our apron denotes that we are encircled by the Holy Wisdom.

Finally, the serpent biting its tail, and thus forming a circle, has always been regarded as the emblem of eternity, and more especially of the Eternal Wisdom of God. Nor must we forget that the snake is peculiarly associated with Shiva, whose close symbolic association with the third degree has already been clearly shown.

Much more might be written on the meaning of the apron, but we cannot devote any more space to this subject, interesting though it may be, although before considering our next point it will perhaps be well to recall what has already been mentioned in the E.A. handbook, viz., that aprons, in addition to their Operative significance, have right through the ages been employed in connection with religious ceremonial.

On the monuments of Egypt a garment, which can best be described as a triangular apron with the point upward, is depicted in circumstances indicating that the wearer is taking part in some kind of ceremony of initiation. In ancient Mexico the Gods are depicted wearing aprons, and it is not without interest to note that the modern Anglican bishop wears an apron, although it appears to have developed from a long flowing robe somewhat the shape of a cassock.

CHAPTER VII.

LEGEND

After the ceremonial investiture of the Cand. the W.M. continues the narrative of the traditional history. At least this is the case in most English workings, but in some Scotch workings the whole story is told first, and subsequently the Cand. and the other Brn. act the chief parts. Perhaps one of the most important points to realise is the correct meaning of the name H.A.B.

Major Sanderson in An Examination of the Masonic Ritual gives the following interesting interpretations, which we will proceed to expand further.-" The title H.A.B. is taken direct from the Hebrew of 2 Chron., Chapter 4, verse 16., and means, ` H. His father.' H. means 'Exaltation of light, their liberty or whiteness, he that destroys'; It is of interest to note that abib in Hebrew means `Ears of corn,' or `Green fruits,' and there is just a possibility that this is the correct title of H."

Bearing these translations in mind we at once perceive a whole series of inner meanings hidden in the name of the principal Architect. Taking the Christian interpretation of our rituals :-firstly, we shall remember that Christ said " If I am raised up (or exalted) I shall draw all men unto me." Secondly, Christ died to make us free, that is, to give us liberty from the bonds of death and hell.

Thirdly, mediaeval divines were never tired of referring to Christ's whiteness and purity, and relate many beautiful legends and allegories to drive home this lesson. One phrase alone will suffice to bring this aspect of the Christ to our minds, i.e. , that He is constantly spoken of as " the lily of the valley." Fourthly, He came to destroy the bonds of death and hell, nor must we forget the old prophecy spoken concerning the coming Christ and the serpent, representing Satan, "

It (Christ) shall bruise thy head, and thou shalt bruise His heel," Gen. 3. v. 15. It is of interest to note that Quetzacoatl, the Mexican Preserver, who fought and overthrew the great giant of evil, was himself smitten in the foot, near to a fall of water, subsequently died from the wound, and ultimately rose again from the grave.

In India Krishna similarly died from an arrow wound in the heel. Moreover, in mediaeval frescoes Christ is constantly represented as crushing the head of the great dragon under His left foot, while in His right hand He upraises a staff on which is a cross. Such scenes are usually described as " The Harrowing of Hell."

Fifthly, if the word abib is the correct rendering for the second half of the name in question, we get a clear reference to the Sacramental bread. The ears of corn are obviously synonymous with the wafer or consecrated bread, which in mediaeval days alone was given to the laity: while the alternative translation, "Green Fruits," brings to our mind the Biblical saying that Christ is "the first fruits of them that slept" (I Corin, 15. 20). Bearing this possible Christian interpretation in mind, installed masters will perceive the deep significance of the P.W. which leads from the degree of M.M. to that of I.M.

But in addition to these Christian interpretations of H.A.B. there was yet another, which in some senses may be regarded as older, and the key to which is supplied by India. In this sense H.A.B. takes on the characteristics of Shiva, the Destroyer.

Firstly, "Exaltation of life" reminds us of the legend that Shiva on a certain day increased in stature until He overtopped the universe, and, as a result, overthrew Brahma, the Creator, and was ackowledged by Vishnu as His superior. On that great day He gathered unto Himself the beginning and the end of all things, Alpha and Omega, and henceforth birth and death alike were in His hands.

Secondly, "Their liberty" refers to the fact that, to the pious Hindu, Shiva by death grants liberty from the toil and anguish of this world, and sets the soul free to mount to greater heights of spirituality.

Thirdly, Shiva is always spoken of as the "Great White God, white with the ashes of the dead who are ever burned in His honour." Nor must we forget that these ashes are always scattered to the four cardinal points of Heaven.

Fourthly, He is in His very essence " The Great Destroyer."

The "Ears of corn" are symbols of Vishnu the Preserver, Who Himself, according to numerous Hindu legends, was slain and rose from the dead, thereby paying allegiance to the Lord of Death ; and so:

Fifthly, we obtain the idea of the Resurrection as symbolised by the ears of corn, which are planted in the earth and bring forth an abundant harvest, the "Green fruits" of the fields. In this connection it is as well to remember that the central theme of the Eleusinian Mysteries was the ear of corn which was shown to the Cand. at the most solemn point of the whole ceremony, and similarly taught the doctrine of the resurrection from the dead.

The next point that strikes us in the legend is the number of craftsmen who "went in search." The Irish version is of peculiar interest, for it relates that it was the twelve who relented who afterwards "went in search," and not a new company of ffiteen. In many ways this is more logical, and certainly has a deep symbolic meaning.

It is logical in that it shows that the penitent twelve did their best to make amends for ever having allowed themselves to listen to the wicked schemes of the other three, and the subsequent decree of K.S., ordering them to wear white gloves and white aprons as a mark of their innocence, is most appropriate. It was a public announcement that K.S. forgave them their indiscretion and acquitted them of responsibility for the crime.

On the other hand, in our version there seems no logical reason why K.S. should order an entirely new batch of F.C.'s to wear these emblems of their innocence, since they clearly had nothing to do with the crime, and moreover, all the others, except the penitent twelve, were equally innocent, and should therefore likewise have been instructed to wear white gloves and aprons. It must be remembered that these white gloves, etc., were not bestowed as a reward for having taken part in the search, but are specifically stated to have been ordered to be worn to denote innocence.

The Irish account goes on to state that the twelve set out from the Temple and went together in one company until they came to a place where four roads met, and formed a cross; then they divided into four companies, and three went North, three East, three South, and three West. Thus they trod the Way of the Cross. In some old Irish workings we are told that the three who went North never returned. This symbolically implies that they went into the Place of Darkness

As the tendency in modern Irish masonry appears to be to adjust its ritual in main essentials to our English workings, it is but fair that I should say that I have a tangible proof of this form of legend, in the shape of an old Irish apron dated 1790, which, unlike modern Irish aprons, has a number of paintings on it depicting incidents in the ritual. One of the paintings shows the twelve F.C.'s separating at the four cross roads. (See frontispiece).

It is clear from all accounts, whether English, Irish, Scotch or American, that the scoundrels, the agents of death, were found by those who went in the direction of Joppa, that is in the W., but we are left in considerable doubt as to whether the b. was found in the E. or in the S.. Symbolically, however, it would clearly be in the S., for H.A.B., like the Christ, was struck down at High Twelve, when the sun is in the S..

From a practical point of view it is fairly obvious that the scoundrels who were carrying away the b. could never have reached Joppa if they had once gone E., for they would have had to fetch half a circle round Jerusalem, a procedure which would have rendered their chance of escape almost hopeless. By going S. they might hope to throw their pursuers off the track, and then turn back at an angle, reach Joppa, and escape by boat. That this was their intention is clear from many old forms of the legend, and especially in those worked in America. King S., however, foresaw this possibility and prevented their escape by forbidding any ships to sail.

In the American working one of the officers of the Lodge enacts the part of a sea captain, and even wears a yachtman's cap. The villains come to him and beg him to take them aboard, but he refused because of the embargo ordered by K.S.. That the same incident was known in the old Irish working is shown by the little picture on the same Irish apron depicting the arrest of the villains on the sea shore, for in the back ground there is a ship.

Let us interpret the meaning of the Irish working first. From the Christian standpoint the twelve F.C's represent the twelve apostles, Mathias replacing the traitor Judas. But in the non-Christian, and possibly earlier interpretation, these twelve would of course be the twelve signs of the Zodiac, searching for the sun which had been eclipsed. We must never forget that in addition to the deep spiritual meaning hidden in our ritual there is also a Solar Myth embedded, which has in the course of years become allegorized and filled with deeper spiritual truths.

But being English masons we must be prepared to find an explanation of the fifteen. In ancient Egyptian times the month consisted of 30 days, and the year of twelve such months, plus five extra days. Now the first fifteen, of whom twelve recanted, presumably represent the first half of that month, while the second half of the month is represented by the fifteen who went in search. But spiritually the meaning of the fifteen is fairly clear. Man has five senses and is triune in nature, and thus implies that Body, Soul and Spirit must cooperate in trying to find God, and employ on that quest their five senses.

Lest there be any misapprehension here I would explain that man is considered to have not only the five physical senses, but also corresponding senses of Soul and Spirit. The phrase "To see with the eyes of the Spirit" is perfectly well known, and similarly we can speak of the eyes of the Soul. To give concrete examples :-Students of psychic science constantly speak of clairaudience and clairvoyance. While it is not necessary to accept this type of phenomena, it is clearly obvious that if man survives death at all his Soul must have a means of communicating with other Souls and that these correspond in some way to our physical senses. In like manner how are we to describe the visions of the great seers and prophets, related in the Bible, except by the possession of spiritual sight ?

Bearing this in mind, we obtain the following interpretation of the fate which befell the three F.C. Lodges into which the fifteen formed themselves. Those who found nothing represent the physical senses of man, which are useless beyond the grave : the next company must therefore represent the Soul, for despite the logic of the physical world, it is the Soul which realises that death does not end all, and so it was one of these who r...d the M But the power which tells us what is right and wrong, and which ultimately punishes us for our offences, is what we call conscience, and thus assuredly is the Divine Spark within us-the Spirit.

Let us now turn to consider the details connected with the dlscovery of the body. The incident of the shrub is such a striking analogy with a similar one found in AEneid, wherein AEneas finds the body of the murdered Polydorus by plucking up a shrub which is near him on the side of a hill, that some students suggest that in the revision of our ritual this incident was copied from Virgil. But, in Who was Hiram Abiff, I show that both refer back to an ancient source and have an allegorical meaning.

One proof supporting this view; is that this particular tree, the Acacia, has from time immemorial been more or less sacred in the near East. In ancient Egypt the earliest forms of the legend of Osiris relate that it was an acacia which grew up round the coffin of Osiris, and not a tamarisk as in the later versions. (See An Examination of the Masonic Ritual, by Major Sanderson).

103

In like manner this tree is sacred in Arabia, India, and many parts of Africa, while it is the Shittim wood of the Old Testament, from which the ark was made. No doubt in this reverence for the acacia we have a survival of the primitive veneration for trees, usually spoken of as "tree and serpent worship." In India the assouata tree is stated to be a symbol of Trimurti, The Three in One. Its roots represent Brahma, its trunk Vishnu, and its branches Shiva, the Destroyer.

At any rate we can regard the acacia tree as in itself an emblem of the resurrection, for the tiny seed which is buried brings forth a mighty tree, covered with fragrant blossoms.

The account of the manner in which the Cas. S...s came into existence, though ingenious, can hardly be taken as historic. As we have already dealt with this point previously, we shall only say that every folk-lore student is well aware that, in the vast majority of cases, legends purporting to explain the origin of a certain custom do not give the real origin at all, but merely indicate that the origin of the custom has been lost, owing to its great antiquity.

The very manner in which some of the S..s are given is sufficient to indicate that they did not originate in the way suggested, while, on the other hand, we find these same S...s all round the world, with entirely different explanations as to their origin. They are indeed ancient landmarks, and the utmost care should be taken not to alter them in any way.

The next incident in the legend is the capture of the scoundrels. In some rituals it is given with much interesting detail of a picturesque nature. All agree that they were apprehended in a tavern, and many say explicidy that it was near the sea shore. Some of the rituals state that the fugitives were overheard lamenting as follows:- "One said, 'Oh, that my t. had been c.a. rather than I should have done it;' while another more sorrowfully exclaimed, `Oh, that my h...t had been t.o. rather than that I should have struck him;' and a third voice brokenly said, `Oh, that my b. had been s. in t. rather than that I should have smitten him,' "

This last version is of interest as explaining the legendary origin of the py. of the three degrees, and incidentally it shows how legend incorporates facts into a story, in order to explain something whose original meaning is lost. It would also appear from this version as if the scoundrels had not intended to actually kill their victim but merely to terrorise him, and in the excitement of the moment lost their heads.

Symbolically this contains a valuable piece of teaching. According to one interpretation the three scoundrels represent "The lust of the flesh, and the lust of the eyes, and the pride of life" (I John, 2. 16). In other words, the sins of the flesh, the sins of the Soul, such as covetousness, and spiritual pride, the most deadly of all.

These sins assuredly destroy man both physically and spiritually, yet it can truly be said that in giving way to them no man intends to destroy himself. From the more strictly Christian standpoint the three scoundrels are Herod,

Caiaphas, and Pontius Pilate, and it is perfectly clear that Pilate and Herod, at any rate, did not wish to kill our Lord; but were caught in a position from which they found it impossible to escape.

Returning to the deeper mystical interpretation we notice that the scoundrels were found in the West, the region of Death, which teaches us that the just retribution for all our sins, whether of body, soul, or spirit, will overtake us after death, and that though in one sense it is God, here shadowed forth by K.S., who punishes, yet in another sense it is our five spiritual faculties which themselves rise up in judgment against us. We ourselves, doom ourselves, and therefore we can obtain nothing but strict justice.

Without pretending that we have exhausted this subject, this brief explanation of the true character of the scoundrels and their captors must suffice, and we will only mention in passing that here also there appears to be a half forgotten astrological reference to the three winter months which oppress the sun.

CHAPTER VIII.

THE TRACING BOARD, ETC.

The next part of the narrative is incorporated in most English workings with the Tracing Board. The most interesting feature is the description of the g.. It is obvious that peculiar stress is laid on the centre, even in the present form of our ritual, because of the way in which the measurements are given. Why should it not have been said that it was six feet long? In some old rituals the g.. or rather the monument, is described as a dome, which made a complete circle at its base, and was three feet from the centre every way.

If so it must have been like a small replica of the earliest form of the Buddhist Pagoda, and the Master was thus buried at the centre. In that case the top of the dome would have been five feet from the surface of the ground, and we should thus get the correct symbolic use of 5 as representing the body, and 3 as representing the spirit, while enabling the human body to be decorously interred. It seems probably that when the g.. was made to conform to the type familiar in England, a desperate effort was made to retain the 3 and 5.

It is worth noting that there is no mention of the use of any c...f...n, despite the picture on the tracing board, and if a c...f....n had been used at the supposed date of the incident it certainly would not have been of the European shape depicted, but much more like an Egyptian Sarcophagus. Nevertheless, though the ritual does not justify the existence of any c..f....n on the tracing board, it was an integral part of the ancient mysteries of Osiris, and its retention in other ritual is almost certainly an ancient landmark.

On the same tracing board may be seen certain letters in the Masonic cypher, which are practically never explained. Very often when transliterated, among other things, they will be found to give the P.W. leading to the three degree. This fact is of interest, for the true meaning of that W., as already explained, is a w...k...r in m...ls, the correct description of H.A.B. The fact that he was buried as near the Sanctum Sanctortum as possible, symbolically denotes that he had reached the centre, and was in union with the Source of All.

The Dormer window historically is the hypostyle, the method by which Egyptian and classical temples obtained light. The pillars of the central nave of such temples rose considerably higher than the roofs of the aisles, thus leaving openings through which the light could enter the building. These, however, were many in number, and it is difficult to justify the apparent statement that there was only one such opening. Symbolically it is intended to represent the means by which the Divine Light penetrates into the deepest recesses of every man's nature.

The squared pavement has already been explained under the section dealing with the mosaic pavement, in the first degree, and our readers are therefore referred to it. Briefly, it indicates that man's progress towards the centre is through alternate experiences of good and evil, darkness and light, mercy and severity, life and death.

The Porch which is the entrance to the Sanctum Sanctorum is the gateway of death.

The working tools, "as in other cases, contain much sound moral teaching of typical 18th Century work, but there is one implement which deserves rather more than passing attention. For what follows I must express my indedtedness to W. Bro. Sir John Cockburn, P.G.D. The s..k...t does not appear to be much in use among Operative masons.

It is used by gardeners, but the Operative mason has other means for marking out the ground for the foundations. This implement has more than a superficial resemblance to the Caduceus of Mercury, and Sir John Cockburn suggests that it has been employed to replace this "Heathen" emblem. For my part, I think this is most probable, for it is clear that at the beginning of the 19th century a deliberate attempt was made to eliminate this emblem from our ceremonies. The jewel of the Deacons in the 18th century was not a dove, but a figure of Mercury, bearing the Caduceus.

A number of these old jewels can be seen in the library of Grand Lodge, and there are still a few old Lodges which continue to use them, instead of the modern jewel. Now this jewel is far more appropriate to the Deacons than is a dove. A dove is the emblem of peace and a carrier pigeon bears messages, but neither of these birds do all the work of the Deacons. Mercury, however, was the Messenger of the Gods, and carried the instructions of Jupiter, thus fulfilling one set of the duties of a deacon.

He was also the conductor of souls through the underworld; taking the dead by one hand, and uplifting the Caduceus in the other, he led the Shade from the grave, through the perils of the underworld, to the Elysian Fields; before his Caduceus the powers of evil fled. In mediaeval escatology it is Christ who leads the Souls on a similar journey, uplifting in His Hand the Cross of Salvation. Even to-day the jewels of the Deacons in a Mark Lodge bear the Caduceus, a mute but convincing witness to the use of this emblem in Freemasonry.

We can thus see that on the one hand a deliberate effort was made to delete from our ceremonies the Caduceus, probably because it was considered to be Pagan, while on the other hand it was clearly quite easy for ignorant masonic furnishers, in the course of years, to make the Caduceus approximate more and more to a masonic tool, so as to fit it in with other avowedly masonic implemens.

As a masonic tool it has very little significance, even to a Speculative, and is of no practical value to an Operative, but the Caduceus would be peculiarly appropriate to the third degree. In short, it is an ancient landmark, an emblem of the dead and forgotten Mysteries, and symbolical of Him who leads the soul from the darkness of the grave to the light of the resurrection.

Before leaving the M.M. degree let me say to all installed masters that if they have received the P.W., not the W. of an Installed master, but the P.W. leading from the M.M. to that further degree, they will find in it evidence not of a mere hint of the resurrection, but of the Resurrection itself, and a close association with the version of that doctrine set forth in the life of the Perfect Master.

CHAPTER IX.

THE CLOSING

Here we are reminded that we are working in symbolism, for we come back from the West, i.e., the grave, to this material world. But we have only obtained substitutes, and we offer them as some consolation to the spirit, i.e., the W.M. The advance to the centre of the room is an obvious reference to the other centre. The s...s are communicated by the body to the soul, which passes them on to the spirit. The meaning of these s....s is dealt with in the ceremony, but it is worth noting that the word shows clearly that the s....t is to be found only through the death of the body.

The actual Hebrew word whose corrupt form we use really means " My son is slain." It is also well to remember that the p.s. and the s. of G.& D. (Scottish form) are, old signs which come down from the ancient mysteries, and are still found throughout the world. A brief summary of that has already been said may be helpful. The p.s. is often associated with Shiva, the Destroyer, and is also found appropriately used at Burobudor in Java; it refers to that occult centre, the solar plexus. In view of what the lost s...t is, this sign is therefore most significant. In other words, it is a hint to those who deserve to know while it conceals from those who do not.

The Scottish sign of G. & D. is found all round the world, and always has the same meaning of an appeal for help. It is used in the most primitive initiatory rites of a boy into manhood, and in Kenya the boy takes it to indicate that he is ready for the operation of circumcision to begin. In Nyasaland, among the Yaos, it is associated with a grave, and in Mexico the Preserver is shown making it. He was slain and rose from the dead, and it is constantly found in Mexico in the form of a carving, consisting of a skeleton cut in half at the centre and making this sign, as, for example, at the Temple of Uxmal.

The manner of communicating the s..s and the gr. are equally old. Indeed, the lion's grip appears to be the grip of all the Mysteries. It was the Grip of Mithra, and by this grip Osiris was raised. Among the Druids it was also known, as is shown by a carving at Iona. I have, however, gone into the evidence for the antiquity of our signs so fully that I will not take up further space here.

We may as well add, however, that the number "5" no doubt refers to the five senses of man, just as the seven steps remind us of the Egyptian sub-division of every mortal.

Having received the sub. s...s the W.M., or Spirit, confirms their use till the true ones are discovered. This last remark indicates that the quest is not ended or abandoned, in reality it has just begun; the first stage only has been passed, which stage is death. It also tells every Craft Mason that he a good craftsman till he has at least taken the Royal Arch.

Thus the spirit acknowledges that death is a step forward. It has freed the soul of the trammels imposed on it by the body, and so our life's work on earth, as symbolised in the Lodge, is closed. The knocks indicate that the spirit now dominates the soul and body and before we leave these heights it is well to point out that almost all the great religious teachers have taught that in some mysterious way this physical body will be transformed, and still be used after death. In short, that matter, as well as spirit, is part of God. Science has shown that matter is indestructable, though its form may be changed completely, and so even after the symbolical death and resurrection, three knocks are still required.

CHAPTER X.

CONCLUSION

This then concludes the third degree. More than any other degree in Craft Masonry it has embedded in it ancient landmarks, brought down from a long distant past. Under the surface lie hidden, meanings within meanings, which I make no pretence to have exhausted. Already this book has exceeded in length either of the two previous ones, but to do full justice to the sublime degree one would require a volume four times as large as this.

I trust, however, that I have given some help, more especially to younger brethren, which will aid them to glimpse the deeper side of Freemasonry. If they too will strive to discover further alternative meanings, I shall feel this labour of mine has been well repaid.

Let me again warn them that just because Masonry is so old, its rituals, in the course of years, have been again and again revised, and newer meanings have continually been grafted on to the old stock. We are not entitled to say one meaning is right and another wrong.

Both may be right. Christianity itself has taken over a vast mass of pre-Christian ceremonies and symbols, and the student is perfectly entitled to consider that both the Christian and the pre-Christian interpretations of these symbols are equally deserving of respect.

There is also another point which should be borne in mind. Again and again we find that incidents and phrases which appear to have come from the Bible, on closer investigation are found not to correspond exactly with the Biblical narrative. At one time there was a tendency to say that in these cases it was our duty to substitute the Biblical version for the "Inaccurate" traditional form.

With all due respect I venture to say that such action is totally unjustifiable. Masonry is not the Bible. It is a traditional ritual into which 18th century revisers inserted fragments from the Bible, because that was the only book dealing with the period of the masonic incidents which was then available to them.

To-day, we know a great deal more about this period than did our 18th century predecessors, and the modern investigator has just cause to lament the well meaning, but misdirected, zeal of these worthy masons, who thereby have probably destroyed for ever valuable landmarks, which would have helped us to discover the historical growth and the symbolic meaning of many parts of our ceremonies.

Such apparent contradictions, and even mistakes, as appear to exist, should be carefully retained, for they are sure indications to the conscientous student of a connection with a long distant past, which modern methods of research may enable us finally to trace to its origin. If, however, they are revised out of existence, future generations will have nothing to help them in the task of unravelling the true history and meaning of Freemasonry.

If a Sn. does not correspond with the explanation of the manner in which it is said to have originated, don't alter the way of giving the Sn., for it is an ancient landmark. Rather try to discover if anywhere in the world that Sn. is still used in some old ceremony which may throw light on its true origin.

If H.A.B. was not buried in a c...f...n, don't eliminate the c...f...n from the tracing board, but rather bear in mind that his great prototype, Osiris, was so buried and that the c...f...n played a peculiarly important part in the legend which recounts his death : which legend was hoary with antiquity before K.S. was born.

Finally, let me say that even if a man can never fathom the full meaning of the third degree, yet there is no man worthy of the name who has passed through that third degree but will certainly have learnt one important lesson, namely, how to d., and thereby will be the better man.

THE HIGHER DEGREES' HANDBOOK

by W.Bro. J.S.M. WARD

PREFACE

In attempting to give an outline sketch of the various degrees in Freemasonry in a book of this description, I am faced by many difficulties, not the least of which is how to write in an interesting way about degrees, which many of my readers have not taken, without giving away more than is permissible.

One of my reasons for writing this book is to encourage Brethren to take these "Advanced Degrees." We still meet Brethren who say that there is nothing beyond the Craft worth taking. As one who has taken all the degrees for which he is qualified, I can state from personal experience that, with one or two small exceptions, practically all the degrees are of the greatest value.

Of course, my readers must bear in mind that a Brother gets out of Masonry in proportion to what he brings into it. If he approaches it with a keen intellectual mind, based on a reasonable amount of study of the meaning of symbolism, he naturally will learn far more than if he approaches it merely from the point of view of a man who knows a good dinner when he eats one, and cares nothing about the meaning of the ceremonies which take place in the Lodge Room.

In conclusion I must express my indebtedness to Messrs. Toye & Co. for the loan of the blocks which illustrate this book.

CHAPTER I.

HISTORICAL SURVEY

The early history of the so-called "Higher Degrees" is even more obscure than that of the Craft, and in consequence a tendency has grown up to regard them as "Manufactured" during the 18th century.

In my opinion this is too hasty a conclusion, for some of these degrees at any rate bear every evidence of antiquity, and contain that wisdom which has been handed down from generation to generation.

The third degree clearly foreshadows a subsequent degree, wherein the lost s...s will be finally recovered, in fact without such a degree the whole of the Craft ceremonies would be meaningless. Moreover, as we shall show later, the most important Higher Degrees use Sns. of great antiquity, which have been clearly handed down from ancient days in precisely the same way as have our Craft Sns., of which full evidence has been given in the History Handbook. There is also documentary evidence to show that the legends of some of these degrees were well known by our medieval ancestors, and actually incorporated in the Ancient Charges. As, for example, the two pillars which were set up before the flood, survived that deluge, and were subsequently re-discovered by masons. This legend forms the theme of the 13th degree of the A. and A. Rite which is called the Royal Arch of Enoch.

The earliest printed references to any of the Higher Degrees are to the Royal Arch in 1741, and to the Royal Order of Scotland in 1743, when it was in such a vigorous state of health that it had a Provincial Grand Lodge in London, with at least two Chapters under its control.

The Higher Degrees appear to fall into three main groups:-(1) Those that extend the story of the Craft; (2) Those which purport to restore the lost S..s; and (3) The Chivalric Degrees. With regard to the first group two tendencies seem to have been at work during the 18th century. The one being to cut out of the Craft various parts of the legend, and the other being to enlarge certain incidents referred to in the Craft stories, add picturesque detail, and evolve out of them a new degree. My own convictio n is that the root matter of nearly all the Higher Degrees comes from traditions and legends cherished by our medieval predecessors.

There is no doubt that all our rituals, the Craft included, underwent considerable revision during the 18th century. In the case of the Craft Degrees a considerable amount of excision was necessitated by the alteration of the clause in the constitution which changed Masonry from a Christian to a non-Christian basis. This process of excision of all Christian references was not completed until the time of the Treaty of Union, in 1813, and one example for England will suffice. Dunckley, in the second half o f the 18th century, declared that the "Blazing Star" meant the star at Bethlehem which guided the wise men to the infant Christ. In Scotland to this day there still survives a distinct reference to the Christ in the Craft Degrees, for the V.S.L. is opened by the D.C. with a quotation from the opening verse of the gospel of St. John, - "In the beginning was the Word," - whilst the Lodge is closed with the following quotation from the same sou rce, "And the Word was with God." Now this clearly indicates the e xistence of a Christian explanation of the lost S..s which, though no longer countenanced in the Craft Degrees in England, survives in such degrees as the Rose Croix.

We thus see that anything Christian was eliminated from the lower degrees, and this explains the probable origin of some of the Higher Degrees. At the same time, the general style of our Craft Rituals has been altered. Apparently in early days the actual part taken by the candidate during the ceremony was comparatively small, and the bulk of the work consisted of lectures, some parts being by question and answer, while other parts contained various legends connected with the Order. Gradually the tendency arose to make the candidate take a more active and dramatic part in the ceremony, and in order to do this legends and incidents which did not immediately connect with the main theme began to be dropped. These parts were prized by the older members, and rather than see them perish they made them into side Degrees, nor are we justified in assuming that they invented the Sn..s to go with these degrees. In the Royal Order of Scotland to-day the bulk of the cer emony consists of questions and answers put by the M. to the Wardens, and include the giving of S..ns at certain points in the catechism, which S..ns, however, are not specifically taught to the candidate. No doubt when similar portions were cut out and became Christian degrees the Sns. went with them, and naturally became tests to prove that a Brother had taken this new Side Degree, which was nevertheless in reality very ancient.

A characteristic example of a degree which has been cut out of an existing craft degree is the Mark, which was almost certainly part of the ceremony of a F.C., although no doubt it has been amplified since it started on its independent career. On the other hand some of the intermediate degrees of the A. and A Rite, such as the Knights Elect of Nine, are merely amplifications of incidents dismissed in a few words in the Craft ceremony. The Knights Elect of Nine relates in dramatic form the apprehension of one of the criminals.

To an entirely different order belong degrees like the Royal Arch, the Royal Order of Scotland, and the Rose Croix. Each of these in its own way claims to be the completing degree, in which the lost s..s are discovered. The explanation in the case of the last two is Christian, in the case of the R.A. non-Christian, whilst their survival indicates the existence of two diametrically opposed traditions. The Christian Degrees represent the solution put forward in Medieval times, whereas the R.A., though now overlaid with Jewish matter taken from the O.T. in the 18th century, has still within it traces of a tradition which goes right back to pre-Christian times, and clearly comes in part from Egypt, and in part from India.

The third group claim to carry on the teaching of the Chivalric Orders of the Middle Ages, and contain evidence of a mystical tradition which was not entirely orthodox. A characteristic example of these degrees is the Knights Templar.

With regard to these Chivalric Degrees, it may at first sight appear difficult to justify the claim of a building guild to be linked in any way with the proudest Order of Chivalry known to exist in the Middle Ages, but those who hastily brush away this tradition ignore certain salient features of the Templar organisation. The Templars contained at least three sections, or sub-orders, within their ranks, i.e., the Knights themselves, the Templar Priests, and the so-called Serving Brethren, among whom were m any Masons.

When the Order was suppressed thousands of Knights escaped the general persecution, and simply disappeared from history. How did they do it, and what became of them? The most reasonable explanation is that they disguised themselves as Serving Brothers and Lay Brothers of the Temple, and were shielded by these humbler members of their own Order, who entirely escaped persecution. I have gone into this question at great length in "Freemasonry and the Ancient Gods," and will therefore content myself by saying here that there was undoubtedly a link between Masonry and the Templars, which is quite sufficient to explain a partial survival of Templar Rites among the Masonic Brotherhood. The Templars certainly had a mystical teaching very similar to that enshrined in Freemasonry, and traces of it can still be detected in the present rituals of the Masonic Knights Templar, despite the fact that they have been considerably revised in the last half century .

CHAPTER II.

THE MARK DEGREE.

Those of my readers who have already studied the first three Handbooks of this series will realise that the true S..s of a M.M. are not restored to them. The real S.. which was lost was comprehension of the Nature of God, and our Third Degree quite clearly indicates that, despite popular beliefs, we shall not be able to comprehend God as soon as we are dead. The Craft degrees, in short, take us through birth, life and death, and shadow forth the Creative, Preservative and Destructive sides of the Deity. The majority of the other degrees either deal with what befalls a man after death, or else endeavour to explain, or fill in, certain gaps in that historic narrative which is the allegorical basis of the Craft Degrees.

The Mark degree in part belongs to the latter group, and is in reality the completion of the Second Degree. Unquestionably a Brother should receive his Mark when he becomes a F.C., and the degree itself still shows strong operative influence.

It is ruled by Mark Grand Lodge, which meets and has its offices at the Temple in Great Queen Street, next door to the Connaught Rooms. All who love the Higher Degrees owe a debt of gratitude to Mark Grand Lodge, which has acted as Fairy Godmother to many of the Higher Degrees which were left stranded after the Treaty of Union in 1813. Indeed, in many cases it has more or less taken them under its wing, and in consequence we shall have to refer again and again to the fact that the Grand Body which rules a particular degree has its Head Quarters at "Mark Mason's Hall."

The Mark Degree has its own regalia and a special jewel, and perhaps our younger Brethren will be glad of the warning that, with the exception of the R.A., no jewels of the Higher Degree may be worn in a Craft Lodge.

The jewel of the Mark Degree consists of a keystone, made usually of white cornelian, on which are engraved certain mystic letters, the meaning of which are revealed to members of the Degree. It is suspended from a blue and red ribbon. The aprons and collars are also made of blue and red silk.

The teaching of this Degree is largely an amplification of the Second, and tells of education and reward for labour. It also contains a dramatic warning against attempting to obtain wages to which we are not justly entitled, and there is a Messianic hint in the fact "That the stone which the builders rejected has become the headstone of the corner." Incidentally the stone is a keystone, hence the origin of the jewel of the degree. Several facts lead us to suspect that at one time the Degree may have been more pronouncedly Christian than it is to-day. We know that it was flourishing as far back as 1760 in Lodges attached to the Ancients, who were unquestionably strongly pro-Christian.

The legend as now given relates to a period in the building of the Temple previous to the tragedy, although there is abundant evidence to show that as late as the time of the formation of Mark Grand Lodge, 1856, many Mark Lodges in the North had a somewhat similar legend to that now used, but associated it with the second Temple instead of with the first.

Mark therefore, is, or should be, really part of our Craft system, and in Scotland Craft Lodges still have the power to confer it, and constantly do so. In that country it is a necessary qualification for the Excellent Master which itself is an essential qualification for the Royal Arch. We shall refer to the Excellent Master more fully when we come to the Royal Arch, but it is desirable to point out that in Scotland Royal Arch Chapters also have the right to confer the Mark Degree, if a candidate has not already taken it in his Craft Lodge.

The Mark, as we have said, is the completion of the Second Degree, and in itself contains what are practically two degrees, namely, Mark Man and Mark Master. There has been much learned controversy as to whether the Mark Master was at one time conferred on a man as soon as he received his Second Degree. Since it is impossible at the moment to decide when the Mark Degrees arose in their present form, all we can say definitely is that so far as documentary evidence goes, i.e., back to 1760, it appears as if there were always the Degrees of Mark Man and Mark Master, and that although at any rate in theory, Mark Man might be conferred on a F.C., Mark Master seems always to have been restricted to Master Masons. In modern times both Mark Degrees are conferred together, and always on a M.M., although the Mark ritual throughout emphasises the connection with the Second Degree.

THE ARK MARINER.

The Mark Degree, or Degrees, also have associated with them, but in a separate "Lodge," the Royal Ark Mariner Degree. This appears to be old "Operative" work, probably built up in the 18th century by genuine operative masons in the North of England, anxious to have some way of distinguishing a real "Working" mason from a "Speculative." The same explanation probably brought into existence the Degree of St. Laurence the Martyr, of which more anon. The Ark Mariner legend relates to the Deluge, and is taken d irect from the Bible. The most interesting features are the use of a stone, instead of the V.S.L., on which to take the Ob.. The reason for this is explained in the ritual, but it may be that we have here a survival of the old custom of swearing on a stone altar, which was the earliest form of a binding oath. There is also some interesting work with a triangle, but in the main it must be confessed that there is not much really deep teaching in the Degre e. It is, however, quite a pretty little Degree, and has many ardent supporters. It is under the direct rule of Mark Grand Lodge.

CHAPTER III.

THE HOLY ROYAL ARCH OF JERUSALEM.

The Mark completes the Second Degree, but to the youngest Master Mason it must be obvious that a further degree is needed to complete the Third Degree.

The genuine S..s were lost; but were they never re-discovered? Moreover, since they were known to three people, why could not the two survivors have appointed a successor and given him the lost S..s? The Royal Arch sets out to give at any rate one answer to the question - "What were the Gen. S..s of a M.M.?"

Briefly, it is a lost W., but that W. conveys in symbolism a most interesting and illuminating explanation of the nature of God. Indeed, the teaching of the Craft may be summed up by saying that it teaches a man his duty to his neighbour, whereas the "Arch" instructs him in his duty towards God. What is the nature of God therein depicted? It is a trinity, but not the Christian Trinity; it is more like the Hindoo Trinity of Creator, Preserver, and Destroyer. It also clearly indicates the union of Body, Sou l, and Spirit, and shows that by that Union we become united with God. Thus, in its very essence the Royal Arch is supremely mystical, and teaches of the Beatific Vision.

The legend deals with the "Discovery" of the lost S..s at the re-building of the Temple after the return from the Captivity. It will thus be seen that the "Setting" of the degree is from the Old Testament, and this fact must be noted, for there is another explanation of the "Lost Word" which is given in some of the other "Higher" degrees, namely, that the "Lost Word" is Christ, the Logos.

But we have not yet obtained an answer to the very natural question, "Why could not the other two, who knew the S., appoint a successor?" The full exoteric explanation, and also how it was that the S.s came to be deposited in a place of security is given in one of the "Cryptic Degrees," to which we shall refer later in this book. Briefly however, three persons were necessary in order to convey it, but in reality, of course, this is symbolism, and implies that Body, Soul and Spirit must be in union before t hey can fully comprehend the Divine Trinity. While, on the one hand, no living man, trammelled by the bonds of the flesh, can really comprehend the nature of God, nor even do so immediately after death, for our souls will not yet be sufficiently evolved, on the other, hand it is clearly taught that our body does not completely perish, but is rather transmuted, even as St. Paul himself says will take place at the day of judgment. This is no doubt a very profound dogma and difficult for us to understand, bu t if we can realise the fact that matter as well as Spirit is in its original a manifestation of God, and therefore a part of Him, we shall perceive that Matter also is indestructible, although its form may change. This fact is perfectly well recognised by modern science.

In the original form of the Royal Arch, which still survives in Bristol, in Scotland, and in America, the Candidate must pass through four veils, which correspond to various spiritual states of existence which lie beyond the grave, each being a little nearer to the Divine Being than was the previous one. The four Veils are coloured respectively Blue, purple, red and white, and at each Veil the Candidate is challenged by a "Guardian of the Veil" who demands of him the W. and Sn. of the previous Veil. This ceremony in Scotland forms a distinct degree known as the Excellent Master, and the Jewel thereof is a pentacle set with brilliants, which jewel, of course, represents, among other things, man and his five senses. The penal S. of this degree is of great antiquity, and is made by Vishnu when in the form of the Lion Incarnation. Vishnu descended to earth to overthrow an evil giant which was oppressing the world, and slew him by disembowelling him. In Scotla nd no English Royal Arch Mason can be admitted to a Scotch Chapter unless he previously receives the Degree of Excellent Master, which degree he cannot receive unless he has first taken the Mark.

The Passing of the White Veil is really an integral part of the Arch ceremony, and the Sn. corresponding to the S.s of the other Veils is one well known to English Royal Arch Masons. It is only after having passed this barrier that the candidate is enabled to obtain the real S.s of an M.M., the ceremony being very similar to our own Royal Arch. In other words, it is only when we have passed through various spiritual stages of existence that we shall at length be able to comprehend the nature of God. The deletion of the Veils from our ceremony has tended to obscure this important lesson in the English form of the R.A.

A slightly different lesson is taught us by the fate of our predecessor in the Craft. He could not have revealed the S. even if he had wished to do so, for it was an experience, and therefore could not be communicated by words to any living man. We cannot go into a detailed explanation of this deeply mystical ceremony in a book of this nature, but a brief explanation of a certain vault which plays a prominent part therein is essential. Like all symbols in Freemasonry it has several meanings, but the two most important are (a), the underworld, or the grave into which man descends at death, and from which his Soul ultimately ascends to realms of Light. (b) The Mystical interpretation is that it is the M.Ch., that dark recess of the Soul, where dwells the Divine Spark.

The jewel of this degree depicts quite clearly the nature of God. The Double Triangle within the Circle and the Point therein, which is represented by the All-Seeing Eye, is the age-old symbol for God. The triangle within the Circle represents the Spirit within the Circle of Infinity, and is peculiarly associated with God the Creator. R.A. Masons will perceive the significance of this fact in connection with the Altar. The Point within a Circle, among the

123

Hindoos, stands for Paramatma, the All-pervading , the Source and End of All. The triangle with the point downwards is the symbol of rain (water) and represents the preservative side of God (Vishnu), while the triangle with the point upward represents fire, whose flames go up to Heaven, and is therefore the emblem of the Destructive, or rather the transformative, side of God (Shiva). This great symbol was sacred to Babylonian, Egyptian and Jew, and had to each the same inner meaning. It is also sacred to the modern Hindoo, and was so to the ancient Mex ican, and indeed is one of the most venerated symbols in the world.

It will thus be seen that the jewel of the R.A., far from being a mere ornament, contains in itself a summary of the sublime teachings of that degree; the more so as it also has a triple tau. With regard to the tau cross, we have already shown in our earlier handbooks that in its origin it was a Phallic symbol representing the Creative power. We shall remember also that we make a tau cross every time we receive the S.s in the Craft Degrees. Thus the M.M. has himself made the triple tau. It is also worth reminding our readers that only those who have passed the chair and actually ruled a Lodge are entitled to wear three tau crosses on their aprons.

As a Phallic symbol it became an emblem of the Creator, and also, in time, of our animal passions, which must be trampled under foot if we are to advance in Spiritual knowledge. By the time we have reached the Arch, symbolically this has been done, and we are reminded of this by the Union of these three taus beneath the triangles, emblems of the spirit. Moverover, though this is essentially a non-Christian degree we cannot forget that there were three Crosses on Calvary.

The presence of the triple tau, after the experience we have had of it in the Craft, shows how carefully each degree leads on to the next, and it also conveys this important lesson. Each degree in the Craft taught the evolution and purification of (I) the body; (2) the soul; (3) the spirit. These three, now in perfect union, rest under the Shadow of the Supreme Being depicted by the Double Triangles. Thus the presence of the tau crosses teaches us that Man will ultimately rest in the Presence of the King of Kings.

In fact the Royal Arch is full of interesting symbolism: the colours of the regalia, red and purple, the shape of the altar, the position of the three Principals, all convey important lessons, but we cannot spare the space in a small Handbook like this to enlarge further on this degree. Nevertheless, one cannot omit pointing out that as in the Craft the W.M. represented the Spirit, the S.W. the Soul, and the J.W. the Body, so do the corresponding officers in the R.A., although here they are no longer separa ted, but are side by side, and in all cases act as one. The reason for this is that the R.A. depicts that sublime state wherein Body, Soul and Spirit are truly one, and are at Peace in the Presence of God - now properly comprehended.

Our readers will thus perceive that no Craft Mason can consider he has fulfilled his duty as a Mason, until he has taken the Royal Arch, for he has not recovered those lost S..s which he has promised to try and find. The regalia includes apron and a sash of purple and red.

CHAPTER IV.

THE CRYPTIC DEGREES.

The Cryptic Degrees are four in number and are ruled by a Grand Council of their own which, however, in reality is in close alliance with Mark Grand Lodge, whose Hall is their Head Quarters.

They are "The Most Excellent Master," "The Royal Master," "The Select Master," and "The Super-Excellent Master," and their legends bridge the gap, historically, between the first Temple and its destruction. The "Most Excellent Master" must not be confounded with the "Excellent Master" which is worked in Scotland and is really the "Passing of the Veils" in the Royal Arch, although it is kept separate and given first. Its Legend, therefore, is associated with the Second Temple, while the "Most Excellent Master" on the contrary deals with the completion and dedication of the first temple. The apron, which is seldom worn, is white edged with purple, and there is a purple collar. The colour refers to the grief felt by the Brethren for the loss of the third Principal, whose chair is vacant. The most striking feature in the Lodge room is a small replica of the Ark of the Covenant. In theory the qualification for the "Most Excellent Master" is only Mark, but as it is always followed by the "Royal Master," for which the Qualification is Mark and Arch, in practice the Cand. must hold both these degrees.

The Royal Master is a most interesting degree, for it shows how the R.A. S..s came to be deposited in the place in which they were subsequently found. Though H.A.B.'s chair was vacant in the "Most Excellent Master," in the Royal Master he is the chief character, and his disquisition on the subject of "Death" is one of the most beautiful pieces of ritual in Freemasonry. The apron in this degree is black, edged with red, but it is seldom worn. The three Principals, however, wear robes similar to those worn by the same officers in the R.A.

The "Select Master," unlike the preceding degrees, has a special jewel of its own, namely a silver trowel within a triangle of the same metal, which is suspended from a black collar edged and lined with red. The apron is white, edged with red and gold, and is of a triangular shape, but in England neither it nor the jewel are usually worn. In Scotland the jewel of the Cryptic Degrees combines the triangle and the trowel, whereas in England we wear the Jewel of the "Super-Excellent Master" to represent all four degrees.

The "Select Master" is supposed to be held in a crypt (hence the name "Cryptic Degrees") which is the same crypt in which the S..s of the R.A. were at a later date discovered. The legend is similar to that of one of the degrees of the Ancient and Accepted Rite, and relates how a well known mason employed by K.S. accidentally intruded into this crypt when K.S. and H., K. of T., were present. The intruder was subsequently pardoned, but the O.G. who should have prevented his entry, was punished in his place. This is undoubtedly an old legend which crops up again in a third degree, namely, the "Grand Tyler of K.S." one of the Allied Degrees. Its symbolic meaning is that those who push their occult investigation beyond reasonable limits, and without the assistance and protection of more experienced investigators, run serious risks.

The "Super-Excellent Master" is short and not very interesting, but it brings the story of the first Temple down to the time of its threatenened destruction and so bridges the gap between the "Most Excellent Master" and the R.A.. The lesson taught is unswerving loyalty to Jehovah. The colour of this degree is crimson, and a crimson collar should be worn. In practice, however, this is worn only by members of the Grand Council. The Jewel of these degrees is a white enamel triangle with the point downwards, that is, the triangle of the Preserver, and is as a rule the only regalia worn.

The most interesting part of this degree is a carpet on the floor with the following design thereon. Inside a square is a circle, within which is a triangle pointing towards the West, and within the triangle is the C. of the C. on which rests an altar, and on the altar is the ark of the covenant. As the "Floor" design is not adequately explained, the following will be of use.

The triangle pointing West is the symbol of the Preserver, and has been adopted as the jewel of all these degrees in England, and it certainly denotes the underlying principle of the series.

(1). The "Most Excellent Master" teaches us that despite the loss of the chief architect God preserved the work of the Temple and it was duly completed.

(2). The "Royal Master" tells us how the R.A.S..s came to be preserved.

(3). In the "Select Master" the over zealous friend of K.S. was preserved from the dire fate which threatened him.

(4). In the "Super-Excellent Master" we are shown how God preserved a remnant of the people because they preserved their faith in Him.

The triangle within a square denotes the Descent of the Spirit into Matter, while the Circle symbolises Infinity - whence the Spirit comes. The point links the Infinite with the emblem for the All-Pervading - it also refers to each individual "Ego."

The whole symbol, therefore, means that God the Preserver descended from Eternity, and entering into Matter became flesh, and He is one with the All-Pervading. It is therefore a most sacred emblem, and the fact that the Ark of the Covenant stands on the C. shows that the New Dispensation arises out of the old, and the Prophetic reference to this fact is emphasised by the real g. which should remind us of Him Who died upon the Cross. Thus this degree has a Messianic, esoteric meaning, often overlooked by t hose who have taken it.

CHAPTER V.

THE ALLIED DEGREES.

Under this heading are grouped a number of different degrees having little in common. In theory the Grand Council which meets at Mark Masons' Hall controls a large number of degrees, including five which are androgamous, but in practice they only work six degrees. At Newcastle-on-Tyne, however, the Time Immemorial Council also works one or two others, including the Royal Arch Knight Templar Priest, a highly mystical and beautiful ceremony.

The six degrees worked in London are not restricted to Christians, and the only qualifications are Mark and Arch. This is despite the fact that St. Laurence the Martyr and the Knights of Constantinople are clearly Christian degrees. Most of these degrees are of secondary importance, but the Red Cross of Babylon and the High Priest are old and important. The degrees are as follows:-

(I). St. Laurence the Martyr. The Jewel is a gridiron, and it is quite possible that it is to this fact that we owe the ribald tales current in the outside world as to what befalls a man at his initiation into Freemasonry. The legend of this degree in reality has nothing whatever to do with Freemasonry, and is well known to every student of Medieval legends of the Saints. The lesson taught is that of fortitude. This degree appears to be a piece of old Operative ritual brought from Lancashire, and original ly worked up into a degree in order to enable a genuine "Working mason" to distinguish other Operatives from "These newfangled Speculatives." (2). The Knights of Constantinople is associated with the Emperor Constantine, and inculcates the useful lesson of universal equality. The Jewel is a cross surmounted by a crescent moon, hardly a happy choice, for it suggests the triumph of the Crescent over the Cross.

(3). The Secret Monitor is very similar to the first degree of the Secret Monitor as worked by the Grand Conclave, and is associated with David and Jonathan. Its presence among the Allied Degrees bears testimony to an unfortunate split which occurred during the early years of the organisation of the Grand Conclave of the Secret Monitor. It is the only degree in English Freemasonry which is under the control of two entirely distinct bodies. The Jewel is a "Hackle" suspended from a crown, and on the ribbon above the jewel is a bow.

(4). The Grand Tyler of King Solomon relates the story of the accidental intrusion of a F.C. into the secret vaults where K.S., K.H. of T., and H.A.B. were met in consultation. The legend is very similar to that related in the "Select Master" though there are interesting variations, in particular. "The Period" of the legend being earlier. The Jewel is the triangle of the Preserver, point downwards, with certain Hebrew letters engraven in gilt upon a black enamel background.

All these degrees are interesting, but can hardly be called really important, whereas the next two stand in quite a different category.

(5). The Red Cross of Babylon is undoubtedly old, and the sixteenth degree of the A. and A. Rite also bears on the same theme, while similar incidents likewise occur in the Royal Order of Scotland. The Degree in historical order follows, and is closely associated with, the Royal Arch and the rebuilding of the second Temple, and in Scotland is actually controlled by the Supreme Royal Arch Chapter. It has many interesting details, but its outstanding feature is the crossing of the Bridge. This, although tr ansformed into a physical and historical bridge, undoubtedly symbolises something quite different. We are here in the region of eschatology and are being told what befalls a man after death. In all the great religions of the world there is a tradition that sooner or later after death the soul must cross a certain "Bridge." Clearly this "Bridge" means the passing from one state of existence in the world beyond the grave to another, and indicates a further advancement of the Soul away from earth conditions and towards God. The Japanese, Chinese, Parsees, Mahomedans, and Medieval Christians, all speak of this bridge. For example, the Parsees say that the mourners must rise at dawn on the third day after the death of their friend and pray for him, for at that hour he comes to the bridge which he must cross to reach Paradise. The bridge spans the gulf of Hell, and in the middle of the Bridge the Soul will be met by a female form. If his life has been good this form will be that of a beautiful woman who will lead him into Paradise, but if his life has been evil it will be a hideous hag who will meet him and fling him from the bridge into the bottomless pit.

In England this bridge was called "The Brig of Dread," and is depicted in a twelfth century fresco at Chaldon Church, Surrey, where it is shown as if built like a saw. Among those attempting to cross it is a Mason with his tools in his hand. It is also spoken of in an old Lancashire dirge which relates what befalls the Soul of the dead man immediately after it has left its dead body.

"When thou from hence away art passed Every night and alle; To whinny-muir thou comest at last And Christ receive thy soule."

"From whinny-muir when thou mayest pass Every night and alle; To 'Brig of Dread' thou comest at last And Christ receive thy soule."

The exoteric lesson of the degree is "Great is Truth," but the hidden reference to the Bridge of Testing which the soul must pass on its journey towards Paradise is the most striking feature. The Jewel is two crossed swords on a dark green background of enamel.

(6). The High Priest, unlike the other degrees, can only be conferred on a mason who has been a 3rd Principal in a R.A. Chapter. It deals with the Priesthood "after the Order of Melchisedic," and the jewel is the triangle with the point upwards, on which is imposed a mitre.

Briefly then the Allied Degrees link the Old Testament with the New, and the most important are the Red Cross of Babylon and the High Priest, although the other four are not without interest.

CHAPTER VI.

THE ANCIENT AND ACCEPTED RITE.

The Rose Croix of Heredom is now regarded as the 18th Degree of the A. and A. Rite, whose total number of degrees is 33, in reference to the 33 years of our Lord's Life. In practice, however, only the 18th, 30th, 31st, 32nd and 33rd are worked in full in England, and the last three are but sparingly conferred.

In America all the intermediate degrees are worked, i.e., 4th to 33rd inclusive, but in England the 4th to the 17th are merely conferred by name. The 18th is worked in full, but the 19th to the 29th inclusive are similarly conferred by name only.

The qualification for the 18th is one year a Master Mason, and for the 30th it has usually been Prelate or M.W.S., the latter being the title of the ruler of a Rose Croix Chapter. The 18th degree is a highly mystical degree and full of the deepest interest, and in England is restricted to professing Christians. In the U.S.A. and on the Continent of Europe, however, it is not usually regarded as Christian, and non-Christians can become members. One school of Masonic research has propounded a theory that t he Rose Croix was originally Roman Catholic, and invented by the Jacobites. Personally, I have, after very careful search, been unable to find any evidence in support of this view, and frankly I cannot conceive of any conscientious Roman Catholic taking part in the ceremonies.

It seems more probable that the degree is due to Rosicrucian influence, and the earliest historic evidence we can find of these mystics shows that they were Lutheran, but it is quite probable that they inherited an earlier tradition. There appear to be references to Rosicrucian doctrines in Dante, and the Commacine Masons carved the Rose and Compasses over their Lodge door at Assisi in the opening years of the 15th century. Moreover, the ancient Aztecs who likewise venerated the cross had a very similar R ite with the same Sn..s and many of the same incidents. Finally, we cannot ignore the fact that Henry Adamson, M.A., in "The Muses Threnodie" written in 1636, says:-

"For we are Brethren of the Rosie Cross, We have the Mason's Word and Second Sight:"

Now this shows an association of the "Mason's Word" with the Rosie Cross. Personally, I think this refers, not to the present 18th degree, but to the Rosy Cross of the Royal Order of Scotland.

It indicates, however, Rosicrucian influence on Freemasonry long before the rise of the Jacobite movements, and is in a poem describing Protestant Perth.

To revert to the 18th degree as we know it to-day, we find it has four distinct sections. The first consists of the conferring by name of the intermediate degrees, and the other sections form the Rose Croix Degree itself.

It is a highly mystical piece of symbolism, and expresses the passage of Man through the Valley of the Shadow of Death accompanied by the Masonic Virtues F.H. and C.. It ends with his final acceptance into the abode of Light, life and Immortality, and with his recovery of the L.W.

The Badge is twofold; on one side it is black, having in its centre a red calvary cross; on the other side it is white, edged with rose colour; on the apron itself is embroidered a Pelican feeding its young, while on the flap is a triangle within which are certain Hebrew Characters. There is a collar which is similarly two faced; on the reverse it is black with three red crosses, and on the front rose pink, richly embroidered. Among the symbols depicted are the crown of thorns and the serpent holding its tail in its mouth, the emblem of Eternity. The jewel which is suspended from the collar is a golden compass extended to an angle of 60 degrees, surmounted by a celestial crown. On the one side is a scarlet cross within the compasses, and beneath it a Pelican feeding its young. On t he reverse the cross is silver, with a silver eagle rising towards the heavens, and on both sides at the joint of the compasses is a rose.

Despite its present Christian setting it appears that this degree in its main details is a very ancient ceremony. All its essential features are found in the Bora Ceremony of the Australian Aborigines, one of the most primitive races still living. In India and China the Sns. of this degree are associated with God the Preserver. In Ancient Egypt certain parts of the Book of the Dead cover the same ground and show the same Sns. in use. The Ancient Aztecs in Mexico appear to have had practically the same c eremony, as already stated, and some of the Sns. which they make have survived among the Red Indians to this day. In Medieval Europe we find constant examples of the use of the two principal Sns. employed, as for example at Coire Cathedral, - in both 12th and 15th century work, - in a fresco at Basle, painted in the opening years of the 16th century, and in a 17th century panelled room now in the Engadine Museum at St. Moritz. Moreover, a certain Sn. associated with the 9th degree of the A. and A. Rite wh ich indicates sorrow is also found side by side with these Rose Croix Sns. in every one of the above mentioned cases in Europe. Facts like these cannot be brushed aside lightly, and preclude us from accepting the view that the Rose Croix was invented in the 18th century. Indeed, the Mexican Codices, which practically show the complete ceremony, are at least two and a half centuries earlier than the date at which it has been suggested that this degree was invented.

THE GRAND ELECT KNIGHT KADOSH

The other name for this, the 30th degree, is Knight of the Black and White Eagle. In Latin Countries it is strongly Templar in tone, and has acquired a sinister significance because in some of the rituals the duty of avenging the Death of Molay, and the other slaughtered Knights Templars, is taught in a dramatic way. Since the chief culprits responsible for the slaughter of Molay and his Knights were Philip, King of France, and Clement, the Pope, this fact is stated to have been utilised to teach the Cands . that King and Church are the oppressors of the People. Probably this inner meaning is by no means so universally applied on the Continent as anti-masonic writers pretend, but in any ease the English Ritual has been purged of any such idea, if indeed it ever possessed it. The degree is an elaborate one, necessitating three chambers and an ante-room when worked in full, and only the Supreme Council itself can confer it. The regalia, which may be worn in Rose Croix Chapters, consists of a broad black sash suspended from the left shoulder, the point fringed with silver bullion, and on it are embroidered the emblems of the degree. These are an eagle soaring towards the sun, holding the Anchor of Hope in his talons; on the extremity is the banner of England and Wales, which is on a red ground three golden lions; this is crossed by the banner of the Supreme Council, and below it is a red cross formed of four tau crosses, usually called the Cross of Jerusalem.

The breast jewel is a cross pattee in red enamel, with the number "30" upon a blue enamel ground in the centre. From a collarette of black ribbon with a silver edging is hung a black double spreading-eagle, surmounted by a crown, and holding a sword in its claws.

The word "Kadosh" is Hebrew, and means "separated" or "consecrated." The remaining three degrees of the Ancient and Accepted Rite are but sparingly conferred, and take the place to a large extent of Grand Rank in other, degrees.

It will be many years before the young mason attains to these exalted heights, and therefore any detailed description even of the regalia is hardly necessary in a Handbook of this nature. As soon, however, as he becomes a Rose Croix mason he is certain to have an opportunity of seeing from time to time members of these exalted degrees, and learning from them as much as he is entitled to know before they are conferred upon him.

The Ancient and Accepted Rite as now organised derives its authority from the charter granted to it in 1845 by the Supreme Council of the Southern Jurisdiction of the U.S.A., but the Rose Croix, Kadosh, the 28th degree, and several other intermediate degrees were fully established and at work in the 18th century, as historic records show, although how much further they date back is still a matter of dispute.

With regard to the intermediate degrees it is a mistake to assume that they are of no value or interest. They vary considerably in merit, but such degrees as the Royal Arch of Enoch, with its clear indication of Rosicrucian influence, and the account of the discovery of one of the Ancient Pillars inscribed with old time learning, (mentioned in the Ancient Charges), is worthy of careful study, and the same is true of several of the other degrees. For this reason I strongly urge all Rose Croix Masons to att end the annual festival of King Edward VII. Rose Croix Chapter of Improvement, which is held in the Spring each year at Mark Masons' Hall, when two of the intermediate degrees are rehearsed in full. This then is the Ancient and Accepted Rite; a great Rite undoubtedly, which is full of mystical lore, and sets out to show its members that the quest of the lost word ends, not at the Temple at Jerusalem, but on Mount Calvary.

CHAPTER VII.

THE ROYAL ORDER OF SCOTLAND

This Order rules two degrees, the Harodim and the Rosy Cross. The Harodim is conferred in a body called a Chapter, and so in this Order a Chapter is below a Lodge. In practice, however, these two bodies are the same.

The Royal Order has many peculiar features, and it is impossible to do it justice in one chapter of this book.

Firstly, we may note that the Order is unique in that it has one governing body for the whole world, and is the only English Masonic body of which this is true. Grand Lodge must always meet in Scotland.

Qualifications, as laid down by the Grand Lodge in Scotland, is five years a Master Mason, but the Metropolitan Provincial Grand Lodge in practice will only admit members of the 30th degree of the Ancient and Accepted Rite. London Masons, who have not attained to that degree, must therefore go to the Provincial Grand Lodge of the Southern Counties, which meets at Windsor.

These degrees are of great antiquity, and, personally, I consider them the greatest of all our masonic degrees. They are not so dramatic as certain others, such as the Order of the Knights Templar, but they have a unity of purpose and an ancient ritual which is full of the most profound mystical teaching.

It is in curious old Border verse, for the most part, and from internal evidence would appear to ante-date our present form of even the Craft degrees, though it clearly presupposes their existence.

From historical records we know that these "Scotch" degrees were at work in 1743 in London, for there is a record of a Provincial Grand Lodge in London, having at least two Chapters under its control, at that time.

The mere fact that there were at least two Chapters of Harodim at work at this date precludes the possibility of the Order having come into existence in 1743, and the fact that it had to travel from Scotland, and then establish itself and spread in London, justifies us in considering that it can hardly be later in origin than the date of the formation of the Craft Grand Lodge of Scotland itself, which was in 1736. Seven years is, I consider, far too short a time to allow a new degree to spread from Scotland to London and establish itself firmly therein, but if we take this date we shall see that the Royal Order takes precedence in antiquity of any high degree. But, in view of these facts, we cannot dismiss lightly the evidence of Henry Adamson's metrical description of Perth, "The Muses Threnodie," written in 1638, practically a century earlier, in which he writes :-

"For we are brethren of the Rosie Cross We have the Mason's Word, etc."

Note. - He uses the phrase "Rosie Cross," the exact title of the 2nd degree of the Royal Order, and adds that "We have the Mason's Word."

Now the Royal Order purports to give its members the lost "Mason's Word."

Therefore, if language means anything, it means that the brethren of the Rosie Cross claimed to have the true Mason's Word, a claim still made by the Brethren of the Rosy Cross of the Royal Order.

My firm conviction is, therefore, that Adamson, who was a M.A. and a clergyman, was a member of the Royal Order of Scotland, and since the style and language of the ritual fits in with this period, or with one even earlier, I consider that the Royal Order goes back to that period at least. In connection with this it is well to remember that the first record of the initiation of a speculative into Freemasonry in England is on the 20th May, 1641, when Robert Moray, "General Quartermaster of the armie of Scotl and," was initiated at Newcastle by members of the Lodge of Edinburgh, who were with the Scottish Army, which had entered England in arms against King Charles.

Moreover, Moray, was "Protector" of Vaughan, the famous 17th century Rosicrucian. If therefore beyond the Craft lay a Rosicrucian Masonic Order, which could only be entered by those who had first qualified as Freemasons, then we can see an excellent reason why Moray, who was clearly interested in Mysticism in general, and Rosicrucianism in particular, should trouble to be initiated into a Lodge despite the fact that the Army of which he was Quartermaster-General was actually on a campaign.

Incidentally, these facts go clean counter to the theory still held by a few students that the Royal Order was Jacobite. Indeed, the closer one studies this Order the less grounds can one find for this view.

In such a case one would naturally look for some reference to the Martyr King himself. Be it noted this could have been done with perfect safety, for in the Prayer Book of the Established Church of England there was, during the Eighteenth Century, a special service in memory of Charles, King and Martyr. Thus the inclusion of reference to the White Rose, or Charles the Martyr, could easily and safely have been worked into this ritual.

Secondly, let us consider the teaching of the degree. Both the Old and the Young Pretender were Roman Catholics; we should therefore expect that either there would be traces of Roman Catholic teaching in the ritual, or at least that care would be taken to avoid anything that would be in direct opposition to the faith of the hero of the Jacobites. Yet, on looking into the ritual, we find certain most significant omissions. There is no mention of the "Holy Catholic" Church, nor of the "Communion of Saints," both relics of medieval days left standing intact in the Episcopal Churches of Scotland and of England, but further, the ritual goes out of its way to declare we shall obtain salvation through Christ only, thus hitting at the doctrine of the Intercession of the Saints, and even says that our salvation is by Faith alone.

Now this is just one of the particular points of cleavage between Protestantism and Catholicism, for the latter always has maintained the necessity of faith being proved by good works. Salvation by faith alone was one of the outstanding tenets of the Presbyterians, and shows clearly that the ritual in its present form is Presbyterian, and emphatically so. Would men who were inventing a degree to foster the Jacobite cause go out of their way to insert phrases which must wound their hero, and many of his loyal supporters?

This aspect is further emphasised by the fact that among all the paraphernalia employed in the degrees there is neither cross nor crucifix, although we find them in other Masonic High Degrees. The omission must be deliberate, for from the nature of the ritual these emblems might well have been employed. Against these facts, no word in the ritual of a pro-Jacobite nature can be adduced, and so I can see no reason for claiming these degrees were made up to help the Jacobites.

The degrees themselves are highly mystical, and take the candidate from the Master Mason stage, through the Old Testament, over the "Bridge," onto the second Temple, and finally trace Christ's life and death, and show that He is the L.W. .

There are clear traces of that outlook on life which is called "Rosicrucian," and so they are good argument for those who claim that Rosicrucianism did influence Freemasonry. Keeping strictly to the Royal Order, we find in it the root matter of many of our Higher Degrees, and it is possible that some of these have been elaborated out of incidents passed over beliefly in the Royal Order rituals.

As some guide I will indicate references to ideas which were probably subsequently developed further, though it is but fair to add that the alternative also is possible, namely, that these degrees also already existed, and had contributed to the ritual of the Royal Order, instead of having simply evolved from them. These are Royal Arch, Mark, Red Cross of Babylon - the latter very clearly - Templar and Rose Croix. In addition there are many sections entirely unrepresented elsewhere in Masonry.

The ritual works mainly by question and answer, as in the Craft lectures, but one significant ritual practice deserves particular mention. At certain times the Brn. travel the reverse way of the Sun. This is correct, for they are then supposed to be in the region of the D - d, and popular tradition has always taught that the ghosts of men go reverse of the Sun.

The Tower too is most significant, and calls to mind a somewhat similar building described in the Mystical and "Chimycal" Marriage of Christian Rosy Cross, translated by W. Bro. Waite.

The Sns. used in this degree are many in number, and every one is of great antiquity and can be found in various parts of the world associated with Heathen Gods and ancient Rites of Initiation. The actual Sn. of the Harodim is to be seen in the ancient Aztec manuscripts, and is shown in a scene on a vase found at Chama, Mexico. This scene clearly depicts a cand. being initiated into a Mexican Rite, and being taught the Sn.. The case is certainly not later than 1500 A.D. and was only dug up a few years ago . In India the Sn. of Harodim is associated with Vishnu the Preserver. In Ancient Egypt it is shown on a fresco from Thebes dated about 1500 B.C., fragments of which are in the British Museum. Numerous examples could be quoted from Medieval work in Europe, for example in the 17th century panelled room known as the "Audience Chamber of the Visconti-Venosta," which is now in the Engadine Museum at St. Moritz, to which we referred in the previous chapter. This room also shows examples of the Sn. attached to the Rosie Cross degree, and, in the corners of it are figures making the Drinking Sn. of the Royal Order of Scotland. These figures are arranged in pairs as if answering each other.

Perhaps, however, the most significant fact of all is that the ritual of the Hung Society in China, known also as the Triad Society, or the Society of Heaven and Earth, is almost precisely the same in its main incidents as the ceremonies of this Scotch Order.

The regalia of the Order is fairly elaborate. It consists of a Garter, star and two sashes, one red for the Harodim, and one green for the Rosy Cross, and an elaborate apron of white, edged with bands of red and green.

Each candidate receives . . . which is supposed to show his characteristic virtue, and which, as a rule, is spelt without any vowels.

This must suffice for the Royal Order, though it deserves far more space.

CHAPTER VIII.

THE KNIGHTS TEMPLAR AND KNIGHTS OF MALTA.

The Knights Templar carry on the tradition of the Medieval Order, and may be regarded as teaching the Christian life in action. How far there is any historical connection between the Masonic Order and their Medieval predecessors is a question on which Masonic students are at variance. The writer considers that a strong probability exists that there is a definite connection, and has given his reasons at considerable length in "Freemasonry and the Ancient Gods."

It is not proposed to go fully into this controversy in this book, since its purpose is to indicate, so far as is permissible, the meaning of the Degrees, rather than their history. Certain facts, however, deserve to be placed on record:

(1) That in England, and still more in Scotland, the Order, though nominally suppressed in 1307 et seq., did not suffer the merciless slaughter of its members which fell upon them in France. Moreover, owing to the fact that Scotland was in open revolt against Edward II., who was supposed to rule it, enforcement of the edicts against the Knights was quite impossible.

(2) That certain branches of the Order - e.g., in Spain and Portugal - unquestionably survived, merely adopting a new name.

(3) The Charter of Transmission claims to carry on the succession in France. That Charter now hangs in Mark Masons' Hall, and if it were generally accepted as genuine it would practically settle the matter. The fact that it anathematizes the Scotch Templars, if it is genuine, would indicate a separate organisation of the survivors in Scotland, and therefore explain whence Scotch and English Templary derive.

(4) The undoubted fact that not only many Knights, but also the whole of the Templar Priests and lay Brothers, some of whom were Masons, were not even imprisoned, points to another possible line of descent.

Be that as it may, the Ritual worked to-day, though it has been revised several times in recent years, contains many curious features which would indicate considerable antiquity.

At Bristol a man may not take the Rose Croix unless he is a Templar, and this supports the theory of those who believe that originally the Rose Croix was the inner working of the Templars. The Royal Order of Scotland also shows clear indications of a connection with Templary, both in the legend of its foundation and in the use of a certain word common to both Orders, and used in no other Degrees.

In view of the fact that the Royal Order has its Knightly Degree of the "Rosy Cross," these points are of special significance.

The Legend of the foundation of the Royal Order is that Bruce, after Bannockburn, created the Degree of the Rosy Cross so as to reward those Masons who had assisted him in the battle, and conferred on them the honour of Knighthood. Now we know that the Templar Knights, instead of surrendering themselves to Edward II. when he sent his commissioners into Scotland to arrest them, joined his enemy, Bruce.

Is it then not probable that Bruce, by the foundation of this new Order, thus rewarded these Templars and restored to them the Knighthood which by the abolition of the old Order had lapsed?

The Ritual as used to-day has undergone drastic revision recently. To give but one example, there appears no doubt that the altar in the East is a modern innovation, beautiful though it is. Formerly there was only a sepulchre, and there are still a few preceptories where the old Ritual is permitted. Even in the modern Ritual members will recollect that they took the O. at the sepulchre, which significantly is in the C., and not at the East.

This is a matter of great importance as we shall see in a moment. In Scotland the Degree is divided into Novice, Esquire, and Knight. In England there are still three points corresponding to these Medieval divisions, though the fact is rather slurred over. If we recollect

(a) The Robe marks the Novice; (b) The Tunic marks the Esquire; (c) It is only the Knight who is invested with the Mantle;

we shall perceive that the Ritual still bears witness to these three stages. The Cup of Remembrance in the U.S.A. is still drunk from an unusual resectable, and is emphatically the Cup of Mystical Death.

The Ritual of the Knight Templar, as we know it to-day, has obviously an exoteric and an esoteric meaning. The exoteric lesson, and a very good lesson too, is that the Christian soldier must have ever before his eyes in his struggle with the world the precepts of the Master - Christ. He must be a good soldier of Christ outside the doors of Temple; he must uphold truth and justice, defend the weak, and set a fine example of chivalrous conduct in his daily life. In short, he must not only profess Christianity but really live it.

It will thus be seen that a candidate would need to be a Christian, even if he was not definitely called upon to defend the Christian faith - which he is. But within this sound practical lesson there lies a high mystical message. We are taught of the Lamb who was mystically slain before the beginning of the world. We enter as a pilgrim striving to escape from the worldly spirit. We dedicate ourselves to Christ at the C., that is to say, in the hidden recesses of our souls.

In that hidden place our past life of sin lies dead, even as the earthly body of the Redeemer lay in the tomb. Therefore, on it we dedicate ourselves, finding that over our dead past rises, as it were, the figure of The Crucified.

Armed with the weapons of the Spirit we go forth on our spiritual journey, and after long and painful travels return victorious from our conflict with the spiritual foes of man. Note the symbolical three years, corresponding with the three years of Christ's life of ministry on Earth.

But after action must come penance and meditation, and above all we must meditate, not merely on physical death, but still more on that greater mystery, the mystical death; and being thus prepared, we must offer our sacrifice. Nay, more, we must be marked with the sign of His sacrifice, but in Christian mysticism we are taught that the true mystic must spiritually crucify himself, even as the Great Master physically suffered on the Cross, and this is the mystical death. Is that last incident in the life of the mystic forgotten in the Ritual of this great Order? Think it over, Brother Knights.

This is veiled language, and as far as is permissible, I have endeavoured to indicate that Masonic Templary has a great mystical lesson. There are countless small points in the Ritual which support this view, but for obvious reasons I have omitted them, e.g., the gradual investiture of the candidate indicates the acquisition by degrees of certain spiritual qualities.

THE KNIGHTS OF MALTA.

If we regard the Knights Templar as one Degree we find that the Order has two, or possibly three Degrees in all. After the K.T. comes the Mediterranean Pass. It is now, practically, merely a passing Degree leading to the Malta, but it has a significance of its own. The sign, to begin with, is undoubtedly old. Major Sanderson found the same sign in use among the Yaos in Central Africa, and it was also known and venerated by the Arabs. In view of the tradition connecting the Mediterranean Pass and the Ma lta Degrees with the Arabs, this fact is obviously significant. Nor, esoterically, can we ignore the importance of the serpent in connection with a mystical journey, and in like manner "The Sea" is a phrase well known among mystics to imply certain spiritual facts, and is always said to lie beyond the mystical resurrection.

To make myself clear to non-mystical readers, let me add that mystical death and resurrection are well recognised stages in the development of the soul of the man who, while still in the body, is striving to reach spiritual union with God. St. Paul says that he died daily in Christ.

When we reach the Hall in which the degree of Malta is to be worked, we pass certain emblems which we are told indicate birth, life, death, resurrection and ascension. These are a symbolic summary of our whole Masonic career from the time we entered the Craft till the time we axe finally made a Knight of Malta. Further, resurrection is a new birth which, in itself, presupposes a new life, and in the mystical world we must, like St. Paul, be prepared to die daily in Christ.

The Malta, then, is a Degree of mystical, not physical resurrection, and the fact is emphasised by the linking up of the symbolical acts with the true history of the old Knights of St. John of Malta. The symbols on the table should be studied with this key, particularly that of the galley which bore the souls to safety though it perished itself. Our body must one day die, but if we have lived aright it will bring our souls in safety to the "Islands of the Blest." This is true whether viewed mystically, or in regard to life in the world of action.

The Sns. used in this Degree are certainly old, and the Pen. most peculiar and significant. It could hardly have been invented in the 18th century. The Sn. in the Templar degree is shown in the room of the Visconti Venosta to which we have already referred, and in the same room are to be seen figures making the Sn. of the Knights of Malta.

The colour of the Templar robes are white with a red cross, i.e., the "Blood of the Lamb," in which we have washed and become thereby as white as snow. But those of Malta are black, with a white cross: out of the black night of the Soul, out of the darkness of mystical death, the cross of Salvation rises, no longer a cross of suffering, but one of resplendent glory.

CHAPTER IX.

THE REMAINING DEGREES.

There still remains another Order of Christian Chivalry and its outstanding feature is that it is the only Order open to English masons which avowedly sets out to give a Christian interpretation of the Craft and Royal Arch. The degrees which constitute this Order are:-

(a) The Knights of the Red Cross of Constantine, and

(b) The Knights of St. John and the Holy Sepulchre.

Like the Knights Templar this Order has its Head Quarters at Mark Masons' Hall.

The Knights of the Red Cross of Constantine teach us the well-known story of how Constantine came to be converted, but the Lecture contains a most interesting reference to the Roman College of Architects, whom I personally regard as the direct ancestors of the Comacine Masons, from whom Freemasonry descends. I must admit, however, that I should require fairly strong evidence to convince me that Constantine himself was a member of one of the Collegia.

But in any case this degree is merely a stepping stone to the really great degree of the Knights of St. John and the Holy Sepulchre. This degree appears to have consisted once of three degrees and even now has at least three "points," in it, though these may be interpreted as corresponding to novice, esquire, and knight. The ceremonies are solemn, dramatic and of deep mystical significance, but their most striking feature is an attempt to explain the Craft and Royal Arch Ceremonies in a Christian sense. While not prepared to admit that this is the only, or even the original inner meaning of these degrees, I do consider that the interpretation given is of a most interesting and instructive nature, and if we realise that all through the middle ages Freemasonry was avowedly Christian, and demanded of its members belief in the essential doctrines of the Church, we shall see that this interpretation is deserving of very great respect.

Since those desirous of obtaining this interpretation can do so by joining these degrees, no good purpose would be served in disclosing the points interpreted, beyond saying that the Architect of the Temple is identified with Christ, and the various incidents in the history of our hero are similarly interpreted in the light of the Christian story. The outstanding fact, however, is that here we are definitely told that our ceremonies have a secret inner meaning and this is the only degree in English Freemasonry, of which I am aware, which does endeavour to give the meaning of the Craft and Arch.

The degrees enumerated up to this point are all that can be called strictly masonic which are open to the average English Freemason, but there are several quasi-masonic Orders, or Societies as they are usually called, which for all practical purposes are masonic, since they require a masonic qualification, and like other masonic degrees work a ritual with special secrets. These we will now consider.

QUASI-MASONIC DEGREES.

The Secret Monitor which works under the Grand Conclave is one of the best known of these Societies, only Master Masons are admitted, and there are two degrees and a Chair degree. Attached to it is the order of the Scarlet Cord, which has no less than seven degrees. The real object of the Secret Monitor is to strengthen the bonds of Brotherhood and enforce the principle that a Brother should, whenever possible, help another Brother. The Conclaves often do possess more warmth than the average London Lodge , but there is not much inner meaning in the ceremonies and no very valuable lessons will be learnt from them.

Of quite a different type is the Soc. Ros. in Anglia. This, like the Secret Monitor, admits none but Master Masons, and its rulers are eminent members of the Craft. There are nine degrees and the higher ones are said to be conferred only for merit. The Order always has a Lecture at each of its meetings on some abstruse subject. The Soc. Ros., as it is affectionately called by its members, claims to have the same objects as the Medieval Rosicrucians, and it seems probable that there is some historical con nection. It is, however, not the only body which puts forth this claim, even in England, but these are in no sense Masonic.

The Soc. Ros. is also linked with the Illustrious Order of Light which works only at Bradford, at present, and with another Order. It is not so much that these orders are under the control of the Soc. Ros. as that the leading spirits in each are closely associated with the Soc. Ros. and that the members of the Orders are derived only from that Society.

CONCLUSION.

Thus it will be seen that practically all the degrees in Freemasonry have a definite lesson to teach, and an inner meaning to their ceremonies. Some, no doubt, are more important than others, degrees but the man who has never gone beyond the Craft has still much to learn. He has made no real effort to recover that which was lost, and therefore has signally failed to make a daily advancement in Masonic, knowledge. If he has not time to take all the degrees, at least let him try to complete his second degr ee by taking the Mark, and obtain one answer to the question of what was lost, by taking his Royal Arch.

If he has done this, and has gone no further, let him still avoid saying "I don't think much of the Higher Degrees" Until he has taken them he is in no position to form any kind of opinion, and after he has done so I feel sure that he will no longer speak slightingly of some of the greatest mysteries of this or any Age.

THE MORAL TEACHINGS
OF FREEMASONRY

by W.Bro. J.S.M. WARD

CHAPTER I.

"A peculiar system of morality veiled in allegory and illustrated by symbols."

The above phrase is often quoted as if it supplied a complete and adequate definition of Freemasonry, but this is a mistake. It occurs in a certain catechism addressed to an E. A. and should be regarded merely as an explanation of Freemasonry intended for the initiate.

Freemasonry is something much wider than a school of purely moral instruction, as becomes manifest when we study the second and third degrees, which to a large extent consist of mystical teaching of a more complex and spiritual nature than that usually designated by the term, "moral instruction."

The true significance of the above quoted phrase lies in the fact that it is given to an E.A., and the first degree teaches the important lesson that spiritual progress is only possible to those who have conformed rigidly to the moral law. Indeed, it is only when the apprentice has satisfied his instructors that he has made himself acquainted with the principles of moral truth and virtue that he is permitted to extend his researches into the hidden mysteries of nature and science.

Now, "The hidden mysteries of nature and science" are clearly something quite different from the principles of moral truth and virtue. These, we are told, form a necessary qualification for advancement in the search for further knowledge, and this fact should put us on our guard against assuming that Freemasonry is a peculiar system of morality, and nothing more.

Let us, however, consider the phrase in more detail, for at first sight it strikes us as unusual in form. Many students have jumped to the conclusion that it indicates that the morality of Freemasons is peculiar, but even a cursory glance through the rituals, not only of the first but also of the second and third degrees, reveals nothing at all unusual in the type of morality taught. It is, indeed, hardly distinguishable from the ordinary code of morality proclaimed by all the various Christian churches.

What is peculiar, however, is that much of it is taught by allegories and symbols instead of by didactic phrases. Not that the latter are entirely lacking, but in so far as they exist they do not fall under the terms of this definition, and although well deserving of study are obviously for the most part 18th century additions.

It is this system of moral instruction which is accurately described as peculiar and it may, indeed, be regarded as almost unique or at least as characteristic of Freemasonry. It is, moreover, especially marked in the first degree, whereas in the second and third degrees, though not entirely lacking, it is clear that we are dealing with a rather different subject, including the nature of God, the initials of Whose name we are supposed to discover in the second degree.

In this book we hope to set forth some of the moral lessons of Freemasonry which are taught by her to the candidates by means of allegories and symbols, but we shall not entirely ignore some of the definite moral precepts declaimed during the ceremony itself, although, as a rule, these require much less elucidation.

It may be argued, however, that it is necessary to prove that moral instruction is given, even in the first degree, by means of allegories and symbols, as distinct from obvious and perfectly intelligible admonitory phrases. This we will proceed to do.

The manner in which the candidate is brought into the lodge is intended to symbolise the fact that man is by nature the child of ignorance and sin, and would ever have remained so had it not pleased the Almighty to enlighten him by the Light which is from above. We are truly taught that but for Divine inspiration and teaching we should not even be able to perceive what is right and what is wrong. This inspiration may come from our own consciences, which are sparks of the Divine Spirit within us, or from t he instruction contained in the V.S.L., but without it we should ever have remained in a state of moral darkness.

Thus at the very commencement of our Masonic career we are taught in a peculiar way, by means of allegory and symbol, that the moral laws are not man-made conventions but Divine commands, which man should be able to recognise as such by means of the Divine Light within him.

This is by no means an unimportant lesson to a world wherein some doubters are loudly proclaiming that there is no such thing as absolute right and wrong, and that all moral codes are but the accumulated experience of past ages as to what is expedient or convenient. To those who would argue that there is no moral turpitude in theft, since no one has any real right to possess property, and that at the most all that can be said is that it is convenient for the community to punish theft, as otherwise the vict im might take the law into his own hands and create a disturbance, the Mason replies by placing his hand on the V.S.L.. Remembering the most dramatic incident in the first degree, he declares that the Divine Wisdom sets forth in that sacred book the definite command, "Thou shalt not steal," for having been taught to look to the V.S.L. as the great Light in Freemasonry, he has no alternative but to accept this as a definite and binding instr uction, disobedience to which must be accounted for before the thron e of God Himself.

In like manner, the first regular step inculcates the important moral lesson that we must subdue our passions and trample the flesh under our feet. In one of my other books* I have shown that

*The E.A. Handbook, published by The Baskerville Press, Ltd.

this st. represents a tau cross, a symbol which stands for the phallus, and that the latter not unnaturally represents our passions, which therefore must be brought into due subjection. In the Lectures this fact is carefully stressed in unequivocal language, for to the question,-

".... what do you come here to do?"

The reply is,

"To learn to rule and subdue my passions, and make a further progress in Freemasonry."

Now it should be noted that the candidate has not had the significance of the f.r.st. explained to him in the initiation ceremony, yet, from the above answer in the Lectures, it is clear that he is supposed to have sufficient intelligence to understand the significance of this piece of symbolism and apply it to his own character.

The above two examples, out of many possible ones, are sufficient to prove that the definition, given, be it remembered, by the candidate previous to his being passed to the second degree, is a true and accurate definition of Freemasonry as revealed to an E. A.. Namely, a peculiar system of teaching morality, based on the use of allegories and symbols. It is thus that today we should no doubt word the definition, but for all that its true significance is easily discernable. Let us then try and discover si milar pieces of moral, as distinct from mystical, instruction contained in our rituals.

CHAPTER II.

"That virtue which may justly be denominated the distinguishing characteristic of a Freemason's Heart - Charity."

It is very significant that one of the first lessons taught to the initiate is charity, and when using this word we must remember that in its original sense, which was still in use in the 18th century, the word charity meant far more than the mere giving of money or relief to a person in distress. This, indeed, is but the outward expression of the true charity, which today can be best translated by the phrase, "Brotherly Love."

Although many of my readers will instinctively turn to a certain incident towards the end of the ceremony as the occasion when they first had the importance of charity forcibly, and somewhat dramatically, impressed upon their minds, as a matter of fact the method of their preparation and the manner of their progression round the lodge were intended to impress this lesson on them at the very beginning of their advance towards the Light. It is as if they were compelled to enact the Part of one of the most pi tiable spectacles in our great cities; some poor, blind, old beggar, dressed in rags, through which his naked flesh can be seen, led by someone eke through the bustling streets, weak and penniless. A figure fortunately seldom seen in all its grim penury in England today, but still common enough in Eastern countries.

That it is intended to convey this lemon and so stimulate our sympathy for others is shown by this answer in the Lectures:-

Ques. "Why were you led round in this conspicuous manner?"

Ans. "It was figuratively to represent the seeming state of poverty and distress in which I was received into M., on the miseries of which (if realised) were I for a moment to reflect, it could not fail to make that impression on my mind, as to cause me never to shut my ears unkindly to the cries of the distressed, particularly a brother Mason, but listening with attention to their complaints, pity would flow from my breast, accompanied with that relief their necessities required and my ability could afford ."

Now it is important to notice that we are definitely told that the manner of progression is intended to make us realise the meaning of poverty and distress in others, and further that we should not merely assist the unfortunate financially, but listen to their sorrows with a sympathetic ear and pour the balm of Consolation into the bosom of the afflicted.

It is often sympathy, not financial assistance, that a brother requires, a fact which was forcibly brought to my mind by an incident which occurred in a lodge I recently visited. A brother rose and said:-

"Many years ago I lived in a boarding house in Bloomsbury and among the other Boarders was a Roman Catholic, who seemed to be a hard-fisted, unsympathetic sort of man, and by profession was a money-lender. One night, however, I obtained an entirely new light on his real character, which left a profound impression on my mind. At 10.30 p.m. there was a knock at the hall door. It was a message for this man who, as soon as he received it, got up from his comfortable armchair, put on his hat, and went out in to the sleet and rain, for it was a vile night. I discovered that he did not return until breakfast time next morning and drew him into conversation that evening. It seems that he was a member of a certain Roman Catholic Society, the members of which took it in turn to visit members of their church who were sick so as to cheer them up. That night he had been summoned to the bedside of a dying man, a stranger, and had remained with him until the e nd. Now brethren, I thought that that was a truly Christi an and brotherly act.

"On the other hand, a member of this lodge has been seriously ill for six months. I knew him long before he was a Mason and because I am an old friend I have visited him. He is now well on the road to good health, but I am sorry to say that not a single member of the lodge, other than myself, has ever been near him or shown the slightest sympathy or interest in him. I suggest that this is not right, and therefore I beg to propose that the following be entered on our minutes:-

"'That, in the event of the illness of any member of this lodge, the secretary shall make a point of ascertaining whether the invalid would like to receive visits from the members, and if so he shall arrange that various members from time to time shall call upon our sick brother in order to cheer him up and evince their genuine interest and sympathy'."

To the credit of the lodge, be it said, the proposal was unanimously approved, and it was clear that the former invalid had not been neglected from mere callousness, but simply because many were not aware of his illness and it had never occurred to others that he would like visitors.

The incident shows, however, a very practical method of putting into practice our protestations of brotherly love, and one which might well be adopted in all lodges. It is useless to preach brotherly love unless we take steps to apply its precepts. In this particular case there was no real lack of sympathy but there was a defect in organisation, a defect probably existing in most lodges, namely, the lack of a link between the sufferer and his friends. The Secretary is the obvious official to supply this link, and he should make it his duty to keep in touch with the various members of the lodge. Then as soon as he learns that one is sick, or in trouble, he should communicate with the other members who, when thus informed, should feel in duty bound to visit the brother and do what they can to alleviate his distress or inspire him with hope and confidence.

It may be thought that the average secretary already has his hands full with the multitudinous duties thrust on his devoted shoulders, and there is much truth in such an objection. This difficulty could be surmounted, however, if the Secretary made it a rule that if any brother be absent from lodge without sending an explanation showing that he is in good health and happy, after the close of lodge he should pass on the name of such a brother to an old Past Master, who would make it his duty to get in touch with the absent one and ascertain whether all is well.

There are many Past Masters who would be only too pleased to have allocated to them a definite piece of work of such practical utility.

We have seen that the lesson of true charity is dramatically inculcated at the very beginning of the ceremony, and so that it shall not be obliterated from the mind of the candidate by the subsequent incidents in the ritual, it is again emphasised towards the end of the ceremony by the test for m. s. As soon as the full significance of this has been explained to the candidate he is told to retire in order to restore himself to his per. c.. The object of this latter procedure is that there may be a distinct break in the ceremony, during which the candidate can meditate on the important lesson thus conveyed to him, before resuming his further course of instruction, while the emphasis laid on the loss of his former comfort reminds him of the feelings of the poor blind beggar whom he has thus symbolised.

In conclusion, let us not forget what the Lectures themselves say concerning charity, for therein we are taught that it is the best test and surest proof of the sincerity of our religion. Moreover, since Charity and Brotherly Love are but different words for the same all embracing sentiment, let us remember that by the exercise of Brotherly Love we are taught to regard the whole human species as one family; high and low, rich and poor; created by One Almighty Being and sent into the world for the aid, supp ort and protection of each other. Hence, to soothe the unhappy, sympathise in their misfortunes, compassionate their miseries and restore peace to their troubled minds, is the grand aim we should have in view.

These are indeed lofty aspirations, and form the very basis of Masonic morality. They are taught to the initiate by means of allegories and symbols as soon as he enters a lodge, with the definite implication that until he has comprehended them he is not properly prepared to be passed to a higher degree.

CHAPTER III.

"That excellent key, a Freemason's tongue which should speak well of a Brother, absent or present, but when unfortunately that cannot be done with honour, and propriety, should adopt that excellent virtue of the Craft, which is Silence."

The above paragraph constitutes the charge at the end of the first section of the First Lecture and inculcates a lesson which is particularly needed in a Society such as Freemasonry. A group of men constantly meeting together are only too prone to indulge in idle chatter and mild scandal-mongering. It is not necessary to assume that when Bro. A relates to Brother B the latest stories he has heard about Bro. C he is actuated by malice. As likely as not he is merely passing the time between lodge and refre shment, and hardly realises that he may be doing a real injury to a brother by passing on some tale which reflects no credit on the victim. It is clear that the reorganisers of Freemasonry in the 18th century realised how easy it was for petty scandals to pass from month to mouth, to the detriment of real brotherly affection, for there is little doubt that the moral lesson that you should speak well of a brother or else remain silent is dramatically tau ght on two occasions during the ceremony.

Soon after his entrance into Lodge the candidate is led to two of the chief Officers, and is only allowed to pass when each Officer in turn is satisfied that the tongue of good report has spoken in his favour. Here at once we have an important hint of this precept, for seeing that the candidate only gained admission because no one spoke unkindly of his past career, he should remember this fact and not speak unkindly of other brethren. If there were any doubt on this point, the similar testing which takes place towards the end of the ceremony would remove it. Therein the candidate is with much elaboration taught the important lesson of Caution; ostensibly it is caution with regard to Masonic secrets, but though, no doubt, it has this object in view, there is hardly an incident in Freemasonry which does not teach more than one lesson at the same time.

Let us then consider what is meant by the secrets of Freemasonry. Obviously, they are something more important than a few test "words and signs whose chief utility, apparently, is to enable brethren to recognise each other. There would be no use in having such signs unless Freemasonry itself contained some hidden secrets which these guarded, and we do know that hidden in her symbolism, particularly in the second and third degrees, is a system of mystical teaching and possibly, even, a certain amount of occ ult training.

But in the first degree we perceive that the main object of the ceremony is moral training, notwithstanding the fact that there are also mystical secrets hidden therein. From the standpoint of moral training, why then this emphasis on the necessity for silence and secrecy, and why should the first section of the Lectures close on this note ?

The explanation is surely that Masonry aims at developing Brotherly Love and in order that this may be achieved one of the first essentials is confidence in each other. If one brother finds that another has been passing on unkind remarks about him, the fact is sufficient to mar the harmony of the lodge and destroy mutual confidence. It is not merely that a trifling incident passed by word of mouth from man to man tends to be distorted and exaggerated, although this is a fact which cannot be denied, but ev en more that as brothers we ought to avoid doing anything which may harm another's reputation or hurt his feelings. At a later date the Candidate definitely promises to keep a brother's lawful secrets, but even thus early in his career the importance of caution and silence when dealing with the affairs of others is impressed upon his mind. Is it not a golden rule that when we cannot speak well of a brother we should at least remain silent ? There may be exceptions to this rule, occasions when we must prote st against a certain line of conduct, but these are far fewer than at first sight one may be inclined to think. Moreover, in a higher degree the duty, if needs be, of reproving a brother is recognised, but that instruction is not given to an E.A., who is only at the beginning of his masonic career and is in the position of a junior among seniors.

It should be noted, however, that while there may be good reasons for reproving a brother to his face, there are none for telling tales about him behind his back, and the very school boy's code which lays it down that one must not sneak shows that Masonry is not unique in stressing the fact that we should speak well of a brother absent or present, but when that is unfortunately impossible should adopt that excellent virtue of the Craft, which is silence. If this were always done much bitterness and bickeri ng which at present disfigures the social life of the world would automatically vanish.

CHAPTER IV.

"Ever remember that Nature hath implanted in your breast a sacred and indissoluble attachment towards that country whence you derived your birth and infant nurture."

This is, perhaps, one of the most beautiful phrases in the first degree and truly depicts one of the most unselfish characteristics of the human heart. In patriotism we have a virtue wherein personal interest plays a smaller part than in almost any other guiding principle of life; in fact, it may be considered as one of the most altruistic of all the virtues.

It is a striking example of that practical commonsense which lies behind Freemasonry that it should thus recognise the important influence that patriotism exerts in every well-balanced human being, while at the same time holding up the banner of an enlightened internationalism.

Freemasons are taught that a Mason is a brother whatever his country, colour or religion, wherein the Craft transcends all frontiers and prejudices, but in the above phrase she acknowledges the fact that every man has a particular affection for his native land. Herein she is both wiser and more human than those idealists who think that man in his present stage of evolution can cast aside affection for his Motherland and replace it by a kind of world citizenship. Indeed, many of these idealists go further and suggest that a man cannot be both a patriot and a good citizen of the world. No view could be more mistaken. If we cannot love our own fellow citizens, whose language we speak and whose ideals we can understand, how can we possibly hope to comprehend the aspirations of men of a different race or religion? To abuse our country and to decry it in the supposed interests of internationalism, merely shows ignorance of the fundamentals of human life.

There are, of course, different types of patriotism, and this virtue must not be made an excuse for narrow-minded bigotry or for an arrogant claim to over-ride the just rights of other races. Such an attitude, even it if resulted in temporary gain to our country, would be bought at a heavy price indeed, since nations, like individuals, have moral obligations and cannot ignore them without prejudice to their spiritual well-being. The true patriot will, in fact, be the better enabled to understand the attitude of a man of another nation if he realises that he, too, has an indissoluble attachment to that country whence he derived his birth and infant nurture.

Our Masonic organisation aptly illustrates the ideal at which we should aim. Every man feels a peculiar attachment to his Mother Lodge. He probably thinks it is the best lodge in the world, but this in no way prevents him from working for the general good of all branches of the Grand Lodge to which he belongs, and in like manner the true patriot, while being loyal to his Motherland, will strive to work for peace and harmony between the various nations which constitute the whole world.

We are, no doubt, far distant from the day when all the nations of the earth will be joined in one vast federation, but we can each and all of us do our best to assuage asperities of feeling between different nations. When we travel abroad and bear fraternal greetings to a lodge and another jurisdiction, even the humblest of us is an ambassador of peace and goodwill, and we may be assured that the members of that foreign lodge will think no worse of us because we show we are proud of being Englishmen, whil e we on our part by a tactful speech, and, above all, by the obvious sincerity of our fraternal feelings, will do much to remove misunderstandings and help to create a focal point of good fellowship for our own native land in the country we are visiting.

This, indeed, is patriotism of the highest order, as well as good masonry.

CHAPTER V

"Be careful to perform your allotted task while it is yet day."

How often in life do we meet the man who says, "I am too busy earning my living to spend time in doing good or helping those less fortunate than myself, but in a few years things will be easier and even if I don't retire from business I shall have more time to devote to others." The tragedy is that that time never comes, for the more a man becomes immersed in his own personal interests the less time does he find for helping others. This, indeed, has been the burden of every teacher since the dawn of man. " Do good to-day, for tomorrow may never come."

It is so easy to put off doing the altruistic deed which our conscience tells us is required but which necessitates some self-sacrifice of time, if not of money. There is much to be said for the maxim of the boy scout, that we should not be content to lie down to rest at night unless we have at least one fresh good deed to our credit, but we should remember that not only is this a minimum qualification, but it is one intended for boys, not men. The Mason, if he is sincere, should strive to do his duty and , if that were possible, a little more than his duty, on every day which he lives.

It may be asked what is our allotted task? Until we have satisfactorily answered that question we cannot successfully perform that task. The simplest answer is to do whatever our hand findeth to do and do it with all our might, not for our own advantage, but to the glory of the G. A. O. T. U. and for the welfare of our fellow creatures. But every mason should consider that as a member of the Craft he has a special piece of work to do. He hopes to be a perfect ashlar in the Temple of the Most High, and e very ashlar in a building has an allotted place and a definite function.

Therefore, as soon as he enters the Order a man should seriously ask himself what task he can perform for the good of Freemasonry. He has stated that he has entered the Order so as to make himself more generally serviceable to his fellow men, and this being so it is clearly his duty to render service in some fashion.

In particular, what service will he give to the Order which has received him? He has a multitude of tasks from which he can make his choice. Will he study the significance of the ceremonies and as he grows older try to teach the younger brethren what they really mean? There is considerable need for a body of men in Masonry who would undertake this task. At present thousands enter the Order and no one gives them a hint as to the significance of the ceremonies or the valuable lessons they inculcate. In con sequence many of these members either drift out of Freemasonry or merely attend it for its social side. If, however, a brother has no aptitude for this line of work but says that the Social side appeals to him, this does not preclude him from rendering valuable service.

Not merely can he be a supporter of the charities, wherein he can do most useful work, both by contributing himself and by keeping alive the active interest of the whole lodge in these charities, but he can extend the social usefulness of the Lodge itself by seeing to it that every newcomer gets to know all the members. In our modern civilisation, with its speed and turmoil, men are often extremely isolated. It is no longer as easy to make friends or to get to know each other intimately as it was in the days when people were born in small towns and lived there most of their lives. In a City like London the members of a lodge often come from far distant suburbs and meet at a restaurant in town, perhaps six times in the year, and unless someone makes it his special task to bring the members into close touch with each other the new initiate is likely to remain a brother in name only, for the rest of his life.

Numerous other tasks will occur to thoughtful readers, and the real value of them depends largely on the fact that a brother has thought them out for himself. Of this we may be sure, that if each of us earnestly desires to find some task to do we shall find it without much difficulty.

Nevertheless, we ought not to be content to restrict our service to members of our own fraternity. After all, we said that we wished to render ourselves more generally serviceable to our fellowmen, and in no way can we enhance the prestige of our beloved Order more adequately than by so acting as to lead the outside world to say "He is always willing to help because he is a mason." Here, again, a fine example has been set by the Boy Scout movement.

Many of my readers must have seen a reference in the papers to the fact that some years ago an American citizen was helped by a boy scout when in difficulty. He did not even find out the name of the boy, but he discovered that the ideal of a boy scout was to do at least one good turn every day. This so impressed him that when he got back to the United States he started a boy scout movement there. Now would it not be a fine thing if we had men coming into Freemasonry because they had found masons so will ing to help that they felt it to be an institution which they would like to support and spread throughout the whole globe? This, indeed, would be performing our allotted task while it is yet day, and at the end of our earthly career we should have no need to fear the night when no man can work.

CHAPTER VI.

"The Common Gavel is to knock off all superfluous knobs and excrescences, and the chisel is to further smooth and prepare the stone for the hands of the more expert craftsman."

Before considering the moral significance of this sentence it is perhaps desirable to point out that the gavel is not strictly the same tool as the mallet or the setting maul. The tool with which the Master and the other Officers keep order is really a mallet. The gavel is the same as the Adze, which was the principal tool used by Asiatic workmen and by European masons up to the close of the Norman period. Norman work in stone was dressed and carved with this implement, and it was the introduction of the chisel in the 12th century which enabled the craftsmen to produce the more finished carvings and mouldings which constitute one of the characteristic features of early English architecture.

The most casual glance at Norman sculpture work shows that it is comparatively rough and shallow, and entirely lacking in the polish and finish of the chisel-cut sculpture of the succeeding styles. Thus the gavel, or adze, is a different tool from the mallet, which is used with the chisel, and the general use of the term "gavel" for the Master's mallet is almost certainly erroneous. The main difference between the two tools is that while the gavel has at one end a cutting edge, the mallet should be cut of f blunt at each end.

The fact that a chisel is given to an E.A. is in itself an anachronism for it is a tool used, not for the squaring of rough stones, but for the finishing of a perfect ashlar, or for the carving of a delicate piece of sculpture. This anachronism appears very markedly in the ceremony itself, for whereas the first degree deals practically entirely with the training of the moral character, we are told that the chisel points out to us the advantages of a liberal and enlightened education. Now it is the second degree which symbolically sets before us the advantages of education, whereby we are permitted to extend our researches into the hidden mysteries of nature and science: thus the work of the gavel must precede that of the chisel.

With a few deft blows of the adze (or gavel) the skilful mason knocks off the rough knobs and excrescences and produces the rough ashlar. It might be possible to produce the same result with mallet and chisel, but it would be slow and laborious, and one would probably produce no better results than with the adze. We are told that the latter represents conscience and it is an apt simile, for conscience enables a man to roughly shape his character, in broad sweeping lines, and to tell in an instant whether a particular course of action is right or wrong. If it is wrong, he must cut it away, otherwise it will form an ugly excrescence on his character.

A very usual figure of speech is, "So and so is a rough diamond." It implies that he is a man of a fine disposition but lacking in those little

159

refinements which go to make a polished gentleman. To acquire this polish it is necessary to apply the chisel, or, in other words, education, and a man spoken of as a rough diamond is so described because he lacks this polish.

Now it should be noted that if the conscience of a man is defective, although you may produce what appears to be a polished gentleman a closer inspection reveals the fact that there is a serious moral defect in his character. In masonic language, the rough ashlar has not been trimmed square, and although the chisel of education has been applied to the block of stone, the finished ashlar, even though the surface be smooth and polished, is not a true square and would prove useless in the building. It may be that one side is longer than the other or that one surface is convex. Whatever be the defects it is not after all a "Perfect ashlar." In other words, we must first apply the gavel of our consciences before utilising the chisel of education.

We now perceive why symbolically it is wrong for the Master to use the gavel. Each man must use his own conscience, it is the very first tool he should apply, and nobody but he can use it, whereas the Master, who represents a spiritual teacher or instructor, may be fittingly described as using the mallet, that is to say, as directing the education of the junior members of the Craft, for it is with the mallet that the skilled craftsman applies the force required for the chisel and controls the direction in which it shall cut.

Although in a masonic lodge it is almost the universal rule that the E.A. should pass to a F.C., in real life it is not the case, and certainly every one is not capable of directing the education of others. This work requires a skilled teacher, one who has himself learnt thoroughly that which he has subsequently to teach, and also possesses in addition the ability to impart the knowledge he has acquired, qualities which are not by any means always found residing in the same person. On the other hand, God has given to every man a conscience, which will enable him to define the broad principles of right and wrong, and although education may do much to assist the conscience, education without a good conscience may prove a curse instead of a blessing so far as the moral development of the man is concerned.

Thus it will be seen that to call the Master's mallet a gavel and to say that it is given to him as a sign of his power and rulership is flatly to contradict the explanation of the working tools in the first degree. Every workman must use the gavel, even if he be only an E. A., and no man hands over his conscience to the control of another, certainly not one who has had the benefit of our Masonic training. On the other hand, the Master is specifically told that it is his duty to employ and instruct the brethren, and if we choose for the moment to regard the brethren as chisels directed by the Master, we shall probably obtain a true picture of the real intentions of our Masonic system.

So far as Operative Masonry is concerned there seems no shadow of doubt that the first tools given to an E.A. were the gavel and straight edge; the latter being merely a piece of wood five feet long, whereby he could mark out a rough square on a piece of stone, which he then shaped with his adze. No craftsman would place in the hands of a beginner a delicate instrument like a chisel, a tool more quickly damaged than almost any other builder's implement.

Nevertheless, although we can cavel at the presence of the chisel among the working tools of all E.A. from the Operative standpoint, there is for all that considerable justification for its presence at this point in a Speculative Lodge. It is exceedingly probable that by education our 18th century revisers were thinking more of moral instruction than of technical, literary, or social training. Although every man possess a conscience, it cannot be denied that definite moral and religious training is necessa ry for the boy, whereby he is helped to perceive more clearly those finer distinctions between right and wrong which, without some such training, might not be so apparent to him. In this sense the chisel may fitly be regarded as a companion tool to the gavel, for it is impossible to draw any hard and fast line between our natural conscience and our acquired instinct of what is right and wrong, since the latter begins to grow within us even before we can talk or run about.

There is one point about both the chisel and the gavel which must ever be borne in mind since it teaches an important lesson to every sincere freemason. Both necessitate friction, and we may almost say, wounding blows, on the raw material. Now this is precisely the effect alike of conscience and of any system of training. It is not always pleasant when our conscience forbids us to do something; it often means losing something we should like to have, something perhaps which seems actually a part of ourselves . Moreover, often it is through coming into contact, we may almost say friction, with other human beings, that our conscience is brought into play or we acquire education.

A solitary man on a desert island would hardly have any occasion for consulting his conscience at all, but one living in a crowded city is constantly brought into conflict with other men and his conscience alone will help him to decide whether his attitude towards them is just and unselfish. In like manner, a baby on a desert island might grow to man's estate but would acquire little real education without someone to teach him, even if he found a box of books cast up from a wreck he could not read them with out being first taught by another human being.

Now one of the great advantages of a lodge is that men rub shoulders with each other and learn that each is not the sole person in the lodge, but that others have their rights and are entitled to consideration. The friendly intercourse possible therein is undoubtedly of inestimable value in helping to mould the character of every member of the lodge. We are taught to subordinate our wills to the general good and to think unselfishly and for the interest of the lodge as a whole, rather than to try each to go our own way careless of the interests of others. In short, we not only polish our own characters but have them polished for us by the other members, while we in like manner render them a similar service. If, therefore, at any time some incident should occur which hurts our feelings or ruffles our equanimity, let us remember that this may be a well-directed blow of The Master Builder, which is intended to remove some excrescence from our character and thereby mould us hearer to the perfect ashl ar.

CHAPTER VII.

"By square conduct, level steps, and upright actions we may hope to ascend to those ethereal mansions whence all goodness emanates."

All through the ages the square has been regarded as the emblem of justice. In ancient Egypt when the gods appear as judges they are depicted as seated on chairs in which a square is carefully portrayed, and even in the ordinary speech of the outside world a square deal is the generally recognised term for a fair and just transaction. It is not surprising therefore to find that this implement plays a prominent part in our Masonic symbolism, in fact it is one of the very first tools to which the attention of the apprentice is directed after he has received the light.

It should be noticed, however, that the three working tools of a F.C. are also the characteristic jewels of the principal officers of the lodge, and since in every degree the candidate passes, as it were, in review before each of them, we immediately obtain a valuable symbolic lesson, namely, that we cannot make progress towards the light save by square conduct, level steps and upright actions.

There is not much difficulty in understanding the significance of the first and last phrases of the above sentences but sometimes there appears to be a little uncertainty as to the exact significance of the phrase, "level steps." This implies that our feet are planted firmly on the ground and therefore that we feel no uncertainty as to the direction in which we are moving, neither will the winds of adversity divert us from our path.

We know also that the level implies that there is a natural equality between brethren, and so in the phrase, "level steps," we are taught that we should go forward side by side with our fellow members, not trying to push the weaker to the wall, in order to achieve our goal irrespective of the claims of others. This fact is more significant than appears at first sight. In real life some men are more spiritually evolved or more intellectual than others, but we are taught hereby that instead of selfishly has tening on, such men should stay and help the weaker brethren, lending to them something of their intellectual ability or their spiritual insight so that they may keep pace with those more richly endowed. This is peculiarly brought out in the way that Officers work in a team for the good of the whole lodge and are promoted in rotation. It is, indeed, a valuable lesson! The spirit of esprit de corps is a high virtue and one which should particularly dis tinguish a Masonic lodge, and the spirit which will lea d a more evolved brother to pause on his journey to help a weaker one is deserving of cultivation. Moreover, it brings its own reward, for such an action is in the highest sense unselfish, and thus further increases the spiritual evolution of the man himself and brings him yet another step along the path which leads to the goal towards which we are all striving.

When we look round the outside world and see how commercial competition has produced a spirit wherein the weakest are thrust to the wall and men say, "Let the devil take the hindermost," we see, that this little phrase conveys, perhaps, one of the most important and salutary lessons needed by the present generation, and gives another example of the truly exalted moral teaching contained in every word and line of our craft rituals.

Indeed, this willingness to slow down one's own spiritual progress to help another is the essence of self-sacrifice, and has been the guiding principle which has inspired all the great spiritual teachers of the world in their efforts to advance the well-being of struggling humanity.

Now it is important to realise that this spirit of self-sacrifice succeeds to "square conduct." In other words, it is only when a man has learnt to be just to his fellow men that he can realise the next lesson, which is that he must be more than just, he must give up his own rights to help others. There would be nothing unjust in his outpacing his companions, but it would be selfish, or at any rate self-centred. For all that, it should be remembered that the square in some measure represents the letter G. , which stands for God, the Grand Geometrician of the Universe, the Just Judge. There are other aspects of the Deity which are perhaps more lofty, but, as the old Jewish teachers perceived, you must first make man realise that God is Just before you can convince him that He is something even greater than this, namely, a loving father.

Once, however, we have realised that God is just and that we are all partakers of the same nature, all equally His children, we shall perceive that we shall hardly be acting justly to our fellow men if we leave them behind in the race, and do not help and assist them so that all humanity may achieve the same goal.

The above facts also help us to understand the significance of the plumb line, itself an emblem of God's unerring justice, for they cause us to perceive that we must show forth the lessons we have learnt by upright actions. Unless we show by our actions in life that we have assimilated these important teachings, our knowledge is but vain, and herein it is interesting to note that the level and plumb rule, or, rather, the plumb line, will themselves form a square, thus showing that these three, symbols are a trinity and may-be refer to the triune nature of the Supreme Being.

We may at any rate feel sure that the brother who acts up to the principle of the square, level and plumb rule will not have laboured in vain in the terrestrial lodge, and on quitting it may reasonably hope that he will be permitted to enter that Temple not built with hands, eternal in the skies.

CHAPTER VIII.

"For even at this trying moment our Master remained firm and unshaken."

Although it is in the first degree that the candidate is made acquainted with the principles of moral virtue, and the second and third degrees are devoted to more recondite researches, yet all three degrees have their appropriate moral teachings interwoven with other allegorical instruction. If we desired to find a word which most aptly summarises the significance of the third degree, we could not find one more suitable than the word "loyalty," although, of course, this does not preclude the fact that othe r moral lessons are inculcated during the ceremony.

The brethren will remember the peculiar nature of the ob. in this degree, which, while containing a definite reference to the f.p.o.f., also contains a specific promise as to the loyalty we should show towards a brother, by respecting his secrets, protecting his good name and maintaining his honour, both in his absence and presence, and in particular by never injuring him through certain of his relations.

Some masons have been inclined to criticise the last clause on the grounds that by implication it releases the Freemason from a like responsibility to the relations of those who are not masons. This, however, is a gross travesty of the truth. The obligation must be considered in its entirety, and not as if each sentence were a separate and distinct command. The promise is one of loyalty to the Brotherhood as a whole, and to every member thereof, as is shown by the great stress laid on keeping inviolate th e lawful secrets of a brother. No one has ever suggested that because a Freemason thus promises to keep a brother's secrets, this implies that he is thereby exempted from a like duty in the case of non-masons. Similarly, every clause in the ob. inculcates the virtue of loyalty, a lesson which is immediately driven home by the dramatic incidents which follow, in connection with the Traditional History.

After all, what is the clearest moral teaching of the incident here related, is it not loyalty to one's duty, to the promises one has made and to Freemasonry itself? This does not mean that there are not more mystical meanings hidden within the story, there undoubtedly are, but the moral instruction is nevertheless of great importance.

Loyalty to duty. It is this which the story teaches us, and my readers may be interested to know that the same theme is taught in the Mahabarata, in the legend of the Last Journey of Yudisthira, which relates how he goes on a long journey which ultimately ends at the gates of Heaven. There he is told that he is welcome, but his dog, who has followed him, cannot enter Heaven, for Heaven is not the place for dogs. Whereupon the Indian king replies that the dog has followed him loyally throughout his lone, wea ry journey, and that to forsake a friend is as vile as to commit a murder. Rather than do such a foul deed he is prepared to give up all hope of Heaven. Immediately on his utterance of these words the dog changes form and stands beside him as Dharma, the god of Duty, and he enters into heaven.

Here, then, we have the same underlying lesson of loyalty to duty, and it should be remembered that the F.C.s who went in search, on a long and dreary journey, were similarly actuated by loyalty to their lost Master, and inspired by a sense of duty.

It is probably no exaggeration to say that among us English people loyalty to duty is considered one of the highest virtues. The pages of our history give countless examples of this fact, and this virtue probably appeals to us more than almost any other. It is therefore fit and proper that the culminating degree of the Craft should emphasise its importance in almost every line in the ceremony.

We must be careful, however, not to give too narrow an interpretation to the word "duty." The ceremony inculcates loyalty in all its aspects; loyalty to our fellow men; loyalty to a sacred trust reposed in us; loyalty to those set in authority over us and, above all, loyalty to the Supreme Ruler of the Universe. The lesson is driven home by the manner in which the opposite vice is depicted. To all right-minded men, treachery is a peculiarly abhorrent defect. Dante places traitors in the very lowest part of Hell and lowest of all places those who have betrayed a benefactor. The three villains in our story are traitors first of all to a brother, secondly, to their Master, and lastly, to their benefactor, for, ex hypothesi, they must have received the F. C. degree from the very man whom they subsequently treated so badly.

There is one important lesson on this subject which is apt to be overlooked, namely, that the opportunity for the display of this virtue seldom occurs except in times of sorrow and defeat. It is when the foemen ring the castle round, the last food is eaten, the last water drunk and the walls are crumbling before the assaults of the attacking party, that the soldier is able to prove his loyalty. It is when false friends forsake a man, when troubles creep in on every side, that the true friend shows himself in his real colours. It is when a cause is lost, when victory rests on the banners of the enemy, when cowards fly and false friends prove traitors, that loyalty shines out as a glimmering ray amid the darkness. It is tragic, but true, to say that the real test of loyalty is usually on the brink of an open grave, and often the loyal man does not live to receive the reward of his virtue in this life, It is, therefore, in some ways one of the most unselfish of virtues, but it leaves behind it a fragrance sw eeter than myrrh and a crown which is truly celestial.

CHAPTER IX

MASONIC PROVERBS, POEMS AND SAYINGS.

The foregoing chapters make no pretence at exhausting the subject. To deal fully with the moral teachings of Freemasonry would necessitate the writing of many volumes, but such is not the purpose of this book. Herein I have endeavoured to elucidate the moral teaching underlying certain well-known and significant phrases in our ritual, hoping thereby to inspire others to attempt a similar task. It is with this purpose in view that a number of the most pregnant passages have been selected for inclusion in this volume. All of them are worthy of the most careful consideration by thoughtful masons, who will find them most valuable themes for short addresses or brief speeches, wherein they can help to instruct the junior brethren, more especially those who are only just passing through their degrees. Let us not forget that a sound moral basis is the very foundation of every religious system, and Freemasonry herself declares that it is an essential qualification for the student who would endeavour to unravel h er more secret teachings.

Moreover, when faced by a critic from the outside world, a brother will often find that an apt quotation will enable him to develop an argument in defence of our Order which, without disclosing Masonic secrets, will enable an honest critic to perceive that Masonry is definitely a force for good in the world.

The inclusion of a few verses of Masonic poetry needs no justification, for they enable a brother to memorise some Masonic ideal and set it ever before his eyes.

Masonic Proverbs, Poems and Sayings.

(1) Right glad am I to find your faith so well founded.

(2) That virtue which may justly be denominated the distinguishing characteristic of a Freemason's heart, - CHARITY.

(3) The practice of every moral and social virtue.

(4) Let me recommend to your most serious contemplation the Volume of the Sacred Law.

(5) By looking up to Him in every emergency for comfort and support.

(6) Ever remember that Nature hath implanted in your breast a sacred and indissoluble attachment towards that country whence you derived your birth and infant nurture.

(7) Let PRUDENCE direct you, TEMPERANCE chasten you, FORTITUDE support you, and JUSTICE be the Guide in all your actions.

(8) Endeavour to make a daily advancement in Masonic knowledge.

(9) Masonry is not only the most ancient, but also the most honourable Society that ever existed.

(10) A Mason's Charity should know no bounds, save those of prudence.

(11) Learning originated in the East.

(12) The Universe is the Temple of the Deity we serve.

(13) The Sun and Moon are messengers of His Will, and all His Law is concord.

(14) To be in Charity with all men.

(15) CHARITY comprehendeth the whole.

(16) The distinguishing characteristics of a Good Freemason are Virtue, Honour, and Mercy, and may they ever he found in every Mason's breast.

(17) You are expected to make the liberal arts and sciences your daily study, that you may the better discharge your duties as a Mason, and estimate the wonderful works of the Almighty.

(18) "There's naught but what's good To be understood, By a Free and an Accepted Mason."

(19) He who is placed on the lowest spoke of fortune's wheel is equally entitled to our regard, for a time will come - and the wisest of us knows not how soon - when all distinctions, save those of goodness and virtue, will cease, and Death, the Grand Leveller of all human greatness, reduce us to the same state.

(20) Steadily persevere in the practice of every virtue.

(21) Judge with candour, admonish with friendship, and reprehend with mercy.

(22) You are to encourage industry and reward merit; to supply the wants and relieve the necessities of brethren to the uttermost of your power.

(23) View their interests as inseparable from your own.

(24) To the just and virtuous man death hath no terrors equal to the stain of falsehood and dishonour.

(25) The posture of my daily supplications shall remind me of your wants.

(26) You are to inculcate universal benevolence and, by the regularity of your own behaviour, afford the best example for the benefit of others.

(27) You agree to be a good man and true, and strictly to obey the moral law.

(28) Practise out of the Lodge those duties you have been taught in it, and by virtuous, amiable, and discreet conduct prove to the world the happy and beneficial effects of our ancient institution; so that when anyone is said to be a member of it, the world may know that he is one to whom the Burdened Heart may pour forth its sorrow, to whom the Distressed may prefer their suit, whose hand is guided by Justice and whose Heart is Expanded by Benevolence.

(29) What you observe praise-worthy in others you should carefully imitate, and what in them may appear defective you should in yourself amend.

(30) We learn to be meek, humble, and resigned, to be faithful to our God, our Country, and our Laws, to drop a tear of sympathy over the failings of a Brother, and to pour the healing balm of Consolation into the bosom of the afflicted.

(31) May all these principles and tenets be transmitted pure and unpolluted from generation to generation.

(32) Q. What manner of man should a free and accepted mason be?

A. A free born man, brother to a King, fellow to a Prince or to a Beggar, if a Mason and found worthy.

(33) Q. What do you come here to do?

A. To learn to rule and subdue my passions.

(34) The tongue, being an index of the mind, should utter nothing but what the heart may truly dictate.

(35) Masonry is free and requires a perfect freedom of inclination in every Candidate for its mysteries. It is founded on the purest principles of piety and virtue.

(36) FAITH.

Is the foundation of Justice, the bond of Amity, and the chief support of Civil Society. We live and walk by FAITH.

(37) HOPE.

Is an Anchor of the Soul, both sure and steady, and enters into that which is within the Veil.

(38) CHARITY

Is the brightest ornament which can adorn our Masonic profession, and is the best test and surest proof of the sincerity of our religion.

(39) To-day we may travel in PROSPERITY; to-morrow we may totter on the uneven paths of Weakness, Temptation and Adversity.

(40) THE BIBLE

The Almighty has been pleased to reveal more of His Divine Will in that Holy Book than He has by any other means.

(41) MERCY

Mercy, when possessed by the Monarch, adds a lustre to every gem that adorns his crown.

(42) Our Mother Earth is continually labouring for our support; thence we came, and there we must all return.

(43) May Virtue, Honour and Mercy continue to distinguish Free and Accepted Masons.

(44) Contemplate the intellectual faculty and trace it from its development, through the paths of Heavenly science, even to the throne of God Himself.

(45)

Let us toast every brother, Both ancient and young, Who governs his passions And bridles his tongue.

(46) May the fragrance of Virtue, like the sprig of acacia, bloom over the grave of every deceased brother.

(47) Our prayers are reciprocally required for each others' welfare.

(48) May all Freemasons live in love and die in peace.

(49) May every Brother have a heart to feel and a hand to give.

(50) May we be more ready to correct our own faults than to publish an error of a Brother.

(51) May we never condemn in a Brother what we would pardon in ourselves.

(52). To every true and faithful heart That still preserves the secret art.

(53) A MASONIC DIRGE.

There is a calm for those who weep, A rest for weary pilgrims found, They softly lie and sweetly sleep Low in the ground! Low in the ground!

The storm, which wracks the winter sky, No more disturbs their deep repose Than Summer evening's latest sigh That shuts the rose! That shuts the rose!

Ah, mourner! long of storms the sport, Condemned in wretchedness to roam, Hope, thou shalt reach a sheltering port, A quiet home! A quiet home!

The sun is like a spark of fire, A transient meteor in the sky; The soul, immortal as its Sire, Shall never die! Shall never die!

(54) So here's to the sons of the widow, Wherever soever they roam, Here's to all they aspire, And if they desire, A speedy return to their home.

R. Kipling.

(55) We met upon the level, And we parted on the square, And I was Junior Deacon, In my Mother Lodge out there.

R. Kipling.

(56) FROM TIME IMMEMORIAL.

From Yucatan to Java's strand We have followed thy trail o'er sea and land. When Pharaoh lived he knew this sign, Brother of mine, Brother of mine.

Where Vishnu sits enthroned on high I noted Hanuman passing by, And as he passed he made this sign, Brother of mine, Brother of mine.

In the ocean of peace I came to a land Where silence broods on an empty strand, Where ancient Gods of carven stone Gaze o'er the waters, still and lone, And, search as I might, I could but find Fragments of wood, which bring to mind Ancient writings of bygone days . . . Whilst on the hieroglyphs I gaze I find that they also knew the sign, Brothers now dead, yet Brothers of mine!

77539835R00095

Made in the USA
San Bernardino, CA
24 May 2018